PRESSURE POINTS

Previous books by David Pollock

- Business Management in the Local Church

- Church Administration: The Dollars and Sense of It!

- How to Raise Funds in the Local Church

- Introduction to Church Budgeting

- The Fundamentals of Church Budgeting

- Budgeting and Forecasting—Beyond the Basics

- Good and Faithful Servants

PRESSURE POINTS

Managing Those Difficult and Challenging Church Financial Issues

BY

David Pollock, MBA

Library of Congress Control Number:		2010912858
ISBN:	Hardcover	978-1-4535-6792-0
	Softcover	978-1-4535-6791-3
	E-book	978-1-4535-6793-7

This book was printed in the United States of America.

On the Web at *www.resourceministries.net*

To order additional copies of this book, contact:
Xlibris Corporation
1-888-795-4274
www.Xlibris.com
Orders@Xlibris.com
85287

CONTENTS

INTRODUCTION

Blest be the tie that binds
Our hearts in Christian love;
The fellowship of kindred minds
Is like that above.

This familiar song is still sung in some churches today as a benediction at the close of a worship service. And oh, if that were only true all the time. But in reality, there are those times when the "tie that binds" is stretched very thin, and the fellowship is not always of kindred minds. And one of the themes that pull at those ties is often the issue of church finances. Aside from the practice of doctrinal beliefs, worship styles, and even how the preacher dresses on Sunday, money and some of the related issues have the potential to cause contention, strife, and what I'll refer to as *pressure points*. These are matters that can become divisive if not handled properly and quickly. To take it one step further, being aware of potential problems before they occur can eliminate uncomfortable and disruptive issues. As the saying goes, to be forewarned is to be forearmed!

The goal of this book is to identify some of the financial pressure points that have been shown to present themselves in local church congregations. Admittedly, this isn't a complete or exhaustive list, but these are some of the problematic areas I have encountered after working with churches for over three decades.

Getting Organized

Pressure point (noun): where problems or difficulties are likely to occur; a situation, matter, or person that presents perplexity or difficulty:

The intention of this book is to address many of the issues that are related to the financial challenges facing a local church. However, one of the basic problems behind many of these "pressure points," as I refer to them, are the manner in which the church is organized. Before we look at specific financial challenges, I am convinced an examination of the way a church is organized could prevent or eliminate some of the difficult financial issues. I have found after many years of working with churches, which is often the case, there is a basic need for churches to simply get organized. Many problems would be solved or could have been prevented if there was an organizational framework, a chain-of-command so to speak. The goal is to handle issues as they rise with a minimum of complexity and effort. Creating an effective line of authority within the church can go a long way toward reducing the number of difficulties. We see this in secular businesses where there are specific people who have defined reporting responsibilities, or there is an approval system in place to permit a checks and balances harmonization.

So let's take a close look at what being organized would look like if it were structured along established basic guidelines.

How the Law Looks at a Church

We all believe that Christ established the church and promised that the gates of hell would not prevail against it. For the believer, that is a well-known, comforting, and unmistakable fact.

Secular society, on the other hand, has different ideas about the church. Without question, throughout history, the true biblical church has often been the subject of scorn and persecution; and sometimes it has simply been ignored.

In North America, it hasn't been persecuted, nor has it endured hardships. Contrary to what some conspiracy theorists say, the IRS is not out to get the churches in America. However, there are signs that there is less tolerance for churches in certain communities. Local ordinances and zoning laws in some situations work against churches. Sometimes the activities of churches are being restricted as a result of the "environmental impact"—that is, traffic flow and on street parking throughout adjoining neighborhoods. Also, the loss of property tax revenue is a factor. If a church acquires a sizable parcel of land, that means land is taken off the tax rolls.

Church leaders need to be aware of how they are viewed in the eyes of the law in order to avoid problems and complications with the "system."

Generally speaking, and for our purposes, a church has two meanings. First, there is the physical description: "a building set apart or consecrated for public worship." Then there's the people-oriented designation: "a group of worshippers: a congregation."

Tax Exemption for Churches

Tax law and IRS regulations do not define "religious." But the courts have defined "religious" broadly. In part, because of these constitutional concerns, some religious organizations are subject to more lenient reporting and auditing requirements under federal tax law.

Although not stated in the regulations, the IRS applies the following fourteen criteria to decide whether a religious organization can qualify as a "church":

- Tax exemption for churches
- Distinct legal existence
- Recognized creed and form of worship
- Definite and distinct ecclesiastical government
- Formal code of doctrine and discipline
- Distinct religious history
- Membership not associated with any other church or denomination
- Ordination of ordained ministers
- Literature of its own
- Ordained ministers selected after completing prescribed course of studies
- Regular congregations
- Regular religious services
- Sunday schools for religious instruction of the young
- Schools for the preparation of its ministers
- Incorporation

A legal definition could also encompass both of these definitions. When a group of worshipers wish to officially establish themselves as a "church," there are two choices facing them right away. Should a church be a nonprofit corporation or an unincorporated association? Legally, a church is not required to be incorporated. However, there are certain advantages available to membership if they do choose to incorporate.

In my capacity as a consultant to churches, I have been asked to explain the advantages and disadvantage of being incorporated. It is surprising to learn that there are a lot of churches who do not wish to be incorporated, although not as many as in the past. Their primary argument is that they don't want to be under the authority of any government that is secular and "man-made."

But there is a flip side to that notion. When I ask them if the contributions to their church are considered tax-deductible, in most cases, they say yes. I then tell them, "No, they are not because that government that they choose not to align themselves with has not given them that privilege. The church has not filed for and been granted tax-exempt status as a charitable, nonprofit organization within their specific state. Furthermore, your church is then considered a business, and you are supposed to be paying income tax. You are in fact breaking the law by withholding taxes due the government. What did Christ say about paying your taxes?"

Incorporating: Disadvantages

The disadvantages of not incorporating are significant. Although some churches refuse to become "entangled in the affairs of this world" and in governmental regulations on philosophical grounds, perhaps they should reconsider their decision.

Incorporating: Advantages

The main advantages are twofold: liability protection and tax exemption. A church that chooses to do business as a corporation has protection from liability. Members are exempt from liability if the leaders or other members engage in any wrongful activity. (This will be discussed in more depth in a few moments.) In the event of a legal action against the church, claims would be paid out of an insurance policy or from the assets of the church, but not from the assets of the members. Under specific circumstances, if an individual officer or person is guilty of wrongdoing, a lawsuit could be brought against that individual; but the remaining members would be free from liability.

On a practical level, it is difficult to do business without incorporating. Banks are reluctant to open accounts without someone's taking ultimate financial responsibility, which could usually mean the pastor. A church functioning as an unincorporated association normally places the pastor or one or more trustees at risk for all debts, contracts, and legal matters. Furthermore, while an unincorporated church cannot sue or be sued, in most states, legal action can be brought against the officers or church members. Lawyers will find the deep pockets and go after them.

So what are the benefits of incorporating? When a church incorporates, it normally secures a nonprofit status within their state. (Not every state provides the exact same benefits to churches.)

The benefits of the nonprofit distinction are many. Once a church is recognized as a nonprofit by an individual state, the federal government will bestow federal nonprofit benefits. But generally, the advantages of being a nonprofit organization that has secured tax-exempt status are several.

Incorporation: Tax-Exemption Advantages
(Under the Internal Revenue Code)

- Its donors can be offered the benefit of a deduction for contributions.
- It can, under certain conditions, benefit from using standard nonprofit postal rates.
- It qualifies for exemption not only from state and local income taxes, but also from property taxes (for property used directly for its exempt function) and certain sales and use taxes as well.
- It may qualify for exemption from the Federal Unemployment Tax Act in certain situations.
- Its employees may participate in 403 (b) tax-sheltered annuities.
- It is an exclusive beneficiary of free radio and television public service announcements (PSAs) provided by local media outlets (normally in smaller communities!).
- It may exclude compensation to ministers from the Federal Insurance Contributions Act FICA social security base.

Nonprofit Status Requirements

When applying for nonprofit tax-exempt status under federal law, churches usually must receive a nonprofit status from their state government. Once this is accomplished, a church could choose, but not necessarily, to apply for the status of a public nonprofit and the designation as a "501 (c) (3) organization." This 501 (c) (3) classification affects both the activities that the church may engage in and the manner in which contributions will be treated.

The Internal Revenue Code defines and sets forth guidelines and qualifications for a nonprofit corporation. These include the drafting of articles of incorporation and bylaws. These documents lay out the legal structure of the church government, along with certain limitations on activities. It is advisable either to secure the services of an attorney when preparing these documents or to thoroughly research the preparation of the text at a local library or through the Internet. Generally speaking, to secure the 501 (c) (3) status from the federal government, your Articles of Incorporation must include the following:

1. Religious purpose clause. Keep it simple and to one sentence. For instance, "This church is formed for the purpose of religious instruction, to meet the physical and spiritual needs of the members and to perform sacerdotal functions." (Sacerdotal? From the fifteenth-century Latin meaning "priestly and to do sacred duties." In our context, it would include marrying, burying, baptizing, preaching, teaching, counseling, etc.)

2. A clause that states that there will be no "propaganda or political activity."

3. A method for disbanding the corporation or a "provision for dissolution clause."

Once the church has satisfactory met all the government's requirements, a letter of exemption will be sent from the IRS confirming 501 (c) (3) status.

It is interesting to note that a church is not required to incorporate in order to gain tax-exempt status from the *federal* government. However, the issues of protection from liability and other corporate benefits should be considered. Again, there are churches that have chosen not to file for 501 (c) (3) status on theological grounds. The primary disadvantage of not being considered a 501 (c) (3) exempt organization is that if a contributor should be audited by the IRS in connection with his or her charitable donations, the church might, on behalf of the donor, be required to prove it substantially meets the IRS criteria. Once a church goes through this process a few times, it might wish to reconsider its objection to federal recognition.

Other churches that belong to a denomination such as Presbyterian Church in America (PCA), Evangelical Free Church, and some Southern Baptist churches don't file for IRS exemption because they are already covered under the umbrella of their national denomination's exemption.

So to summarize, to be recognized as a church under IRS rules, there are certain limitations and requirements.

Incorporation: Tax-Exemption Limitations and Requirements (Under Internal Revenue Code)

- A church must be engaged "primarily" in qualified charitable or educational endeavors.
- There are limitations on the extent to which it can engage in substantial legislative activities or other political activities.
- There is a prohibition against private inurnment or private benefit.
- Upon dissolution, the church's assets must be distributed for one or more exempt purposes.

Governmental Requirements

General Reporting

If a church does not have a qualified church business administrator on their staff or on their board as an elder, deacon, or trustee, it should avail itself of the services of a competent CPA to ensure the proper filing of documents with government agencies. I cannot emphasize this enough. Ignorance is no excuse when you are dealing with various governmental departments.

For instance, I know of a church that didn't file for their property tax exemption correctly each year. They failed to declare the pastor's house, the parsonage, which was located on the church property, as exempt. No one thought to tell them it was. They paid thousands of dollars in unnecessary taxes because of this oversight.

County

It may be necessary to comply with county or local property tax laws if you have been exempted from property tax. This is normally done on an annual basis. Failure to file for exemption will usually mean an automatic tax bill, which means the church will have to refile for exemption.

State

Many states require churches to file a form on an annual basis informing them of the names of the church's officers, as well as the individual to contact for legal purposes. This is often done through the state corporation commission or the secretary of state.

There are other requirements for churches that could involve workers' compensation insurance. However, in most states, churches are exempt from paying unemployment taxes. Moreover, state disability tax requirements vary from state to state. California, for instance, currently does not require churches to pay this.

There could also be forms you have to fill out if your employees are subject to state (also city and county) income taxes.

Federal

If the church has paid employees, it is subject to state and federal labor, withholding, and other tax laws. Compliance is required and is not an option for churches.

Churches are unique in that they have privileges no other institution receives from the government. Pastors too are very unusual as to the benefits they are entitled to. For instance, they may opt out of the Social Security system at the beginning of their ministry as long as it is for matter of conscience.

Pastors can designate a portion of their salary as what is called a housing allowance. It's a quirk in the tax code that exempts a portion of their compensation from income taxes, but not Social Security taxes.

Although it may seem like the government places a lot of burdensome rules and regulations on churches, it should be kept in perspective. On balance, no other nation in the world provides as many benefits and an exemption for religious organizations as does the United States. Sometimes we forget some of the freedoms granted to churches.

Christ recognized the distinction between political and spiritual responsibilities when He said, "Give unto Caesar what is Caesar's and to God what is God's" (Matthew 22:21, NIV). As long as laws do not inhibit clear, unmistakable biblical teaching regarding the mission and mandate of the local church, churches need to cooperate with the government and obey the rules.

Legal Structure of a Church

When a church body files for nonprofit status, it must create a "corpus," a legal body or entity. And that body must meet certain requirements. The most basic requirement is as a formal organization that arrangement is to contain officers. Now I realize corporate officers sound a little too businesslike, but as you will see, it serves a very practical purpose.

Board of Directors

Every nonprofit corporation is required to have a board of directors. Within the church setting, this board of directors could be a board of elders, a deacon board, a presbytery, a council, or even trustees. If the highest ruling board is trustees, we will address this later because in most situations, they have a dual role: governing and/or managing.

A board is required to have at least three positions.

Chairman, Vice-Chairman, and Secretary/Treasurer

Ideally, you would want to have four positions: chairman, vice-chairman, secretary, and treasurer. The secretary's position should be separate because this person actually ratifies or approves the actions of the rest of the board members. For instance, if the church wants to open a checking account at the local bank, the bank will want the board secretary to be the one who guarantees that all the people who are allowed to sign checks against the church bank account are in fact authorized. It is the secretary's signature they look for first. If you have ever served on a board, you might have noticed that people are reluctant to be the secretary. This is because this person must be at every meeting, start to finish. And they are the one who takes the minutes of the meeting. This means that they have to reduce board decisions down to brief accurate sentences. Sometimes that can be very challenging, but important and necessary.

Being a member of a church board brings with it certain specific requirements and obligations. For the most part, board members are selected for a variety of reasons. Many churches believe that the board members who hold positions that are found in the New Testament need to be qualified based on what the scriptures say in 1 Timothy and Titus. These would be the biblical offices of an elder or deacon. While the position of deaconess is not found in the Bible, the position of wife of a deacon is mentioned, and there are qualifications listed for these women.

In those churches that delegate ruling authority to trustees, the qualifications are often based on faithfulness in involvement in the church and are more secular in nature. Skills such as experience in facility maintenance or construction, accounting, legal, fund-raising, or finance would be sought in the selection process.

Whatever the highest ruling body may be, nonprofit corporate law requires officers be appointed and identified.

Purpose Statement

It is my firm belief that this ruling board needs to be clear on what its purpose is to be within the church structure. If it sees itself as managing the affairs of the church, then it should seek people to serve on the board who have skills and experience in "management." That is to say, the type of people to recruit on these boards should be able to answer the question "What do you bring to the table that would advance the ministry of our church?" That is a fair question to pose to a prospective board member of a "management" type board.

On the other hand, if the board sees itself in the role of "governing" the church, then the qualifications will be less "skill set" oriented and directed more at the person's character, their ability to make wise decisions and to conform to biblical qualifications. The duties will be more directed at the philosophical—or policy-oriented functions and less toward the functional aspects of the church.

Boardsmanship Style: Governing and Managing

There are those boards, therefore, that are designed to "govern." They operate to use the metaphor at a higher "altitude," one at which they deal with matters of doctrine, philosophy of ministry, vision, etc.

The managing board model, on the other hand, flies at a lower altitude, say a thousand feet, since they deal with operational functions. Neither is wrong nor less important because it depends on the needs and circumstances of the church. Based on their "altitude," they would have different perspectives and, of course, different tasks. Ideally, however, you would want to have two boards, one that governs and one that manages. It cannot be emphasized strongly enough though that a ruling board needs to have a purpose statement: they need to know who there are and where they are going. How high do they plan to fly? How hands-on do they intend to be involved in the operations of the organization?

A church's board can go a long way toward helping the church grow, or they can have the opposite effect. Assuming growth is the desired result, there are three general stages of growth a church will encounter as a result of the actions of the board.

The *Organizing* Board and Staff

— Often consists of close friends
— Adopts an informal decision process
— Has no written plan or strategy
— Gets a lot done (board is involved in daily operations)

The *Governing* Board

— Knows the need for policies and procedures
— Oversees and not manages
— Handles strategic planning, doctrinal issues, and overall direction

The *Institutional* Board and Staff

— Large community-minded board that looks outward
— Is committed and multilayered in terms of staff
— Is a good model for some very large churches, but poor for small to medium size

In addition to the growth factors, there are also challenges to growth: control issues based on "founder's syndrome." The mind-set of "We've always done it this way!" can cause a church to become frozen in the past.

- Failure to think strategically, "minefield" mentality, more focused on where you are stepping than where you are going
- Moving from "reactive" to "proactive" oversight, doesn't anticipate issues and make provisions for them prior to their occurrence

Primary Duties of the Board

The highest ruling board of a church, depending on the policy of the church—that is, a board of elders, deacons, presbytery, and so forth—has essential and basic duties. Every board of a church or nonprofit organization has the same set of responsibilities. They are as follows:

Duty of Care

The duty of care describes the level of competence that is expected of a board member and is commonly expressed as the "duty of care" that an ordinary prudent person would exercise in a like position and under similar circumstances." This means that a board member owes the duty to exercise reasonable care when he or she makes a decision as a steward of the organization.

Duty of Loyalty

The duty of loyalty is a standard of faithfulness; a board member must give undivided allegiance when making decisions affecting the organization. This means that a board member can never use information obtained as a member for a personal gain, but must act in the best interest of the organization.

Duty of Obedience

The duty of obedience requires board members to be faithful to the organization's mission. They are not permitted to act in a way that is inconsistent with the central goals of the organization. A basis for this rule lies in the public's trust that the organization will manage donated funds to fulfill the organization's mission.

Trustees

Within every church, there is a group of men and often women who act as the trustees. Every denomination or independent church has their term for these volunteers who serve under the ruling board. If, as was suggested, the ruling board adopts the "governing" model of leadership, then these people will have the responsibilities of carrying many of the physical requirements of the church.

The work of trustees will vary according to the structure within which the church operates. In many instances, they are the ones who handle the legal matters. They sign documents and act as the agent for the church.

Generally speaking, trustees are the individuals who are responsible for the physical and financial resources of the church. Often, they will have close oversight over five areas:

- Finances
- Buildings and grounds
- Legal/risk management
- Personnel/volunteers
- Long-range planning of physical resources

Areas of responsibility not normally handled by trustees but covered by the spiritual leaders would be the following:

- Interpretation and application of the scriptures and doctrine
- Programming
- Worship/music
- Outreach/missions
- Counseling
- All areas of instruction

Usually, you would place people who have skills or backgrounds that are specific to the committees on which they serve. For example, if you have a CPA available, they would be suited for the finance committee. People in the building trades would work well on the building and grounds committee.

This position, however, has a high level of confidence; and therefore, the people serving in this capacity should be selected carefully. Ideally, the qualifications of a trustee would include the following:

- Is the individual a church member?
- Is he/she technically qualified or have background experience in any of the areas of responsibility assigned to them?
- Are their own personal finances in order?
- Do they have the correct motive for serving on the board?
- Do they understand the difference between being an "owner" and a "manager"? (They are managing someone else's property and money!)

Volunteers

Every believer is gifted to serve God, and scripture tells us that every believer is expected to serve God in some capacity based on their God-given gifts and abilities. Furthermore, every believer must be given opportunities to serve the kingdom of God somewhere, somehow.

Volunteers within the local church are truly the backbone of the ministry. While the pastors may occupy the up-front, more-public positions, it is the volunteers who make everything work.

Matching volunteers with specific areas of service is very important. If you were compelled to hire someone to do the volunteers job, wouldn't you try to make the qualifications fit the job requirements? Of course you would. But there are so many needs in a church and generally, there is someone in the congregation who can meet that need.

I have found that it is very important to match a volunteer's abilities with the task. However, there are those times when someone with a master's degree will be asked to lick envelopes, and that's OK. Often, there are volunteers, although highly qualified in other fields, who enjoy doing lesser, more-simple tasks. If these projects are done in groups, just the fellowship and interaction with friends in itself can be rewarding and in a sense fulfilling.

On the other hand, if, for instance, you have a volunteer who is proficient in computer graphics, a specific and valued skill, you might consider finding a task that suits their capabilities.

However, a word of caution is needed here. If you find a volunteer who has an exceptional skill, be very careful to not rely totally on them to fulfill duties you might otherwise rely on paid staff to do. I am not saying you should avoid this dependency, but you need to have a backup plan just in case that person for whatever reason is not available. Remember, they are volunteers, not paid employees. They are giving their time and do not have an obligation to perform these tasks as would an employee. I am speaking from experience when I say do not place all your eggs in one basket!

Staying in the Loop

Satisfying the Need to Know

A point of contention often experienced in churches with a paid staff is the need to keep the lay leaders, specifically the board of directors, informed. The type or style of the leadership structure will determine how much or how little information is relayed on to the ruling board. There is the obvious need, however, to provide the board with credible information in the amounts they are comfortable with. This is especially true of financial information. As was previously discussed, too much information could create gridlock, and too little might result in misinformed decisions. Therefore, the staff and, in some cases, lay leaders need to help the board of directors make good decisions by providing them with appropriate facts and information.

Good board oversight depends on enlightened decision making. Board members, in turn, need to be knowledgeable about the church's status and needs if they are to make sound decisions that advance its mission. But boards often say that the information they receive hinders rather than facilitates good oversight and strong leadership. They protest that they are overwhelmed with large quantities of irrelevant information, or they don't get enough information, or they receive material too late to devote serious attention to it. An effective system of the flow of information between the board and staff should have a suitable balance.

An example would be in the need to make adjustments to budgets. This problem was discussed earlier, but it is a genuine pressure point when it's not clear what and how much latitude a staff member has in altering the budget line items or to shift funds around within a department's budget.

Types of Information

Management expert Dr. John Carver describes three types of board information:

- *Decision information* is used to make decisions, such as selection criteria to measure staff performance.
- *Monitoring information* enables the board to assess whether its policy directions are being met. It looks to the past and provides a specific survey of performance against criteria. An example is an annual review of the church's goals and, if available, the strategic plan.
- *Incidental information* is for general information of the board and not related to action. It falls under the category of providing information to inform, but not to require a decision.

Too often, board information is primarily incidental information. Although such material is useful in maintaining an overall impression of the church being managed, it is not usually specific enough to help board members make decisions or monitor the church' success at carrying out its ministry.

Establishing a System

Establishing and maintaining a board information system is the joint responsibility of the board chairperson, board members, the senior pastor, and staff members who work with the board. The board should discuss:

- what information it needs to do its job,
- how often it wants the information, and
- in what form it needs the information.

Given this feedback, the staff can establish content, format, and frequency of information they will provide the board.

Characteristics of Good Board Information

Barry S. Bader, a consultant and author specializing in board governance, identifies seven guidelines for developing effective board information:

- Concise: Is the information communicated as quickly as possible?
- Meaningful: Is the information presented in a relationship to a significant factor, such as a goal set by the board, past performance, or comparative date?
- Timely: Is the information relevant to the current agenda?
- Relevant to responsibilities: Does the information help the board discharge its responsibilities? For example, if the church has an annual audit, are they provided with the results in accordance with their fiduciary responsibilities?
- Best available: Is the information the best available indicator of the situation or condition being described? Can better information be provided?
- Context: Is it clear why this information is important?
- Graphic presentation: Could the information be presented better graphically than in words?
- Basic contents of a board information system

Every board must decide for itself exactly what information it needs. For most churches, however, the following list could be a starting point.

At least two weeks before each meeting:

- Agenda
- Information about issues for discussion when appropriate
- Committee reports

At least two weeks before the board meeting at which the topic is discussed:

- Annual budget
- Annual report
- Strategic plan

After each board meeting:

- Minutes
- Notice of next meeting

Monthly:

- Financial report
- Significant published articles about the church, if any, or church newsletter
- Ministry progress reports

Quarterly:

- Report from the senior pastor summarizing current activities, his perspective on the overall ministry of the church, accomplishments, and needs
- Advance copies of publications, brochures, or promotional material

Annual Report

Keeping staff and board members in the loop will go a long way toward eliminating the pressure points of misinformation, a lack of information that leads to misunderstandings. Let's see what we can do to keep the channels of communication open and clear

Financial Reporting

How Transparent?

Transparency, the lack or abundance thereof, is in vogue these days. We hear about the need for top executives of failing corporations to make their compensation packages known. And the same is said of the salaries of senior pastors of large churches or the heads of huge media ministries. In fact, some of these pay packages and perks are the subject of exposés on the local evening news; and of course, the reports never seem to have a positive spin.

Much of the heat generated by these stories is based on legitimate concerns. But sometimes people take this account and transfer them back to their own local church. Outsiders often hurl accusations at ministers of churches, claiming they are "in it for the money." And they point to the latest scandalous report in the local paper. There isn't much we as "insiders" can do to combat that perception when there are in fact a few bad apples out there sullying the reputation of those who don't preach the Gospel for personal gain.

More to the theme of this book, which is identifying and dealing with financial pressure points, common questions asked in many churches in this regard are as follows: How much of the church's finances should be made known to the congregation and even the community? And if made public, how detailed should these revelations be? Should the salaries of the paid staff public be made known too?

There is something we can do, though, to address this issue; and that's to report the financial resources of our churches in a manner that is open, honest, and professional. And that can begin with the method by which we report our finances and demonstrating what good stewardship looks like.

A Different Perspective

There is reluctance, however, on the part of many church leaders to make a full discourse of the ministry's finances. They are concerned about what people will do with the information, what conclusions they will draw, or what people will think about the way the leaders are managing the funds. But what leaders may not be aware of is that donors have a moral right to know how their donations are being used. While churches are under no legal requirement to disclose their finances to church members, the moral right still exits. In turn, churches have an ethical duty to inform donors of their finances. Whether a ministry acknowledges and then strives to fulfill this ethical and moral duty is a matter of integrity. As for the donor, the right to know is an aspect of his or her stewardship. To expect a donor to adopt an attitude of "I am loyal to my church, whether they are right or wrong" is not an exercise of good stewardship on their part. Continuing to support any church for that matter that is deliberately not forthcoming with financial information demonstrates a lack of care on the part of the donor. In other words, the donor's stewardship depends on whether he or she has been given the right information and about the ministry.

Psalm 24:1 says, "The earth is the Lord's, and everything in it, the world, and all who live in it." Even though people may earn through their labors the title to a specific amount of money, God remains the ultimate owner of everything because He owns both the world and people. Accordingly, our relationship to property is that of a steward of God, not unlike that of a park ranger. In a sense, we hold the property in trust for the Creator. Our duty is to care for the property God has given us.

The most important principle, therefore, is that God wants both the donor and those who are charged with managing those donations within the church to apply all property to a proper and appropriate use. When either of these two parties fails to do this, they violate their stewardship duty.

The stewardship of any gift is measured by how well the donor sees to it that the gift is put to good use. Wise church leaders, therefore, will work to help its donors to be good stewards. Donors should be told enough information to know whether funds are being put to a use to further God's kingdom by the church. After all, the donor's stewardship is a function of knowledge. The church should communicate why it needs funding and how those funds will be put to use. To further assist the donors, the church should demonstrate its own good stewardship. This is accomplished through the disclosure of financial reporting methods.

Financial Reports

More than one U.S. president has begun a major public address by saying, "Let me make this perfectly clear!" With the advent of computerized accounting programs, we can now make the finances of the church also perfectly clear. Producing financial reports is now available at a touch of a button. Over the years, I witnessed the transformation of accounting, bookkeeping, and reporting procedures transformed and the evolution from documents manually produced with a pencil and a typewriter to the automatically generated reports of today. There is really no excuse for a church not to have professionally appearing accurate financial reports.

However, before we address the extent to which these reports should be made available, let's examine the basic reports themselves, or what could be referred in this case to as "source documents," because it is the accuracy and timeliness of these documents that could constitute the format for reporting to various levels of a church congregation. That said, there are certain individual groups within the church that should have access to detailed reports, and then there are others who should be given reports that are simple and to the point.

Two Essential Reports

There are two financial reports that are fundamental: the Profit and Loss Statement and the Balance Sheet. For the "bean counters" reading this book, yes, I realize there are other reports you would believe are necessary. However, I'm attempting to keep this simple and focus on the overarching issue of what is an appropriate report based on the intended audience.

Profit and Loss Statement

In most business settings, a profit and loss statement, commonly referred to as a P&L statement, is a very important document. (See a sample at the end of the chapter.) Often, these reports are produced for public consumption; that is to say, outside organizations require them before doing business with a church. For instance, banks or major suppliers of goods or services will want to see the church's financial statement before extending credit in any form.

The P&L shows all the activity related to the income and expenses of the church. However, when you are in a leadership position within an organization, you need to know how the income and expenses compare with what has been budgeted. Therefore, there is a common variation on the P&L statement called budgetary profit and loss. This document is an extension of the traditional P&L in that it shows a comparison between the church's income and expenses versus what was budgeted for each of these areas. The document is normally not a requirement when dealing with outside businesses. The advantage of this report is it shows the total of the actual income, the total of the actual expenses, and a line that shows the net total of the two areas. It subtracts the expense from the income to determine whether there is a surplus or a loss. It also compares each actual line item with what was budgeted for the line item. Most computer programs will then give you the option of selecting what is called a variance, which is the difference between the columns. This may be shown as either a percentage or a dollar value.

The totals shown on this report normally are zeroed out at the end of the year since the budget is normally projected for twelve months. A question often comes up regarding money collected and held for special projects or events. For example, what if the church ends its fiscal year in July, but funds were collected in June for an August camp? Is that money zeroed out, in other words "lost," too? No, it would be carried forward into the next fiscal year and would appear on the new P&L.

So the budgetary profit and loss statement gives you an idea about actual income and expenses compared with what was budgeted for income and expenses. This report is excellent for tracking the income and expenses of a church compared with what was projected. The budgetary P&L also serves as a control mechanism by showing how various ministries are managing their budgeted funds. Without this report being accurate and produced promptly at the end of each month, spending could easily drift and exceed income to a point where a negative cash flow situation would occur. If this report is not made available to the appropriate staff or church members, then suspicions can creep into people's minds. It only takes one person to ask "where the money went" to create a perception and a pressure point that there is something to hide or that funds are not being handle properly. So why not produce a professional, accurate, and up-to-date report to the people on a previously established finance committee to avoid any suspicions? Nip it in the bud, so to speak. It's a question of credibility and—there's that word again—transparency.

Balance Sheet

The next report is called a balance sheet. (See a sample at the end of the chapter.) A balance sheet is an accounting statement showing the amounts and nature of an organization's assets, liabilities, and fund balances on a given date. It shows what you own. Again, with the advent of computerized accounting programs, this report can be updated every time a transaction moves through the software program.

This report is very practical for a church because under nonprofit accounting rules, the balances or the amounts remaining in specific funds are revealed. For example, let's say the church collected money specifically earmarked for a short-term mission trip to the Philippines. The amount raised was $10,000, but the church spent only $8,000. When you go to schedule another trip the next year, you can look on the balance sheet and see that there is still $2,000 remaining. The profit and loss statement won't show that because it is only for a twelve-month period, or a fiscal year.

The balance sheet also shows what the church's net worth is by listing all the assets and liabilities. Under assets, there are current assets and fixed assets. Current assets usually are comprised of cash in checking and savings accounts and funds deposited in reserve or investment accounts.

Fixed assets are items that are purchased that may have a value in excess of a certain amount. For instance, if your church buys an electronic keyboard for $1,000, it would be listed on the balance sheet as a fixed asset. That is called capitalizing a purchase—which brings up a question: Will the keyboard always stay on the balance sheet as being valued at $1,000? No, it would actually lose or depreciate in value. There is an officially established fixed asset depreciation schedule that requires certain items to lose their value at a predetermined rate. This predetermined rate is referred to as the useful life of an asset.

For instance, for buildings and furniture, it's ten years, for vehicles, five years, and for computers, three years.

By depreciating assets, it is possible that an item purchased four years ago will no longer appear on the balance sheet since its initial value has been depreciated. Accounting rules require items to lose their value whether they actually do or not. The original value of the item purchased is determined at the time of the purchase and not necessary when it was new. For instance, if you bought a Ford van five years ago for $20,000, it may only be worth $1,200 if you were to try to sell it today. The value is based on the trade in value, which is determined by what is called a Kelley Blue Book, the auto industry guide to automotive vehicle valuation.

In accounting practices, however, there is what's called the useful life of an asset. And it has been established that a Ford truck depreciates to zero or 20 percent in five years. What if you bought that truck today for $1,200? You would start the five-year clock all over again because you acquired an asset for $1,200. The useful life guideline is for accounting purposes even though that five-year-old truck may be running just fine with a new paint job and tires. The point is some sort of guidelines needs to be established.

The interesting point is that normally, a building in most areas of the country under normal circumstances increases in value. Many of us who bought homes in Southern California and held them for over ten years probably couldn't afford to purchase the same home today because of the appreciation of values. Again, the assumption is all assets have a useful life; and therefore, their value decreases. As illustrated with the Ford truck, if I were to purchase my home today, I would have to what is called book the value at today's cost.

Heavenly Valley Community Church Budgetary Profit and Loss
FYE 200_ /200_

	Actual	*Budget*	*Variance +/-*
INCOME			
4101-Offerings	368,500	365,000	3,500
4102-Other Income	9,856	9,000	856
	13,781		
	392,137	374,000	4,356
EXPENSE			
5000-Compensation			
5010-Senior Pastor	45,000	45,000	—
5011-Adult Ministries	40,000	40,000	—
5012-Music Minister	40,000	40,000	—
5013-Youth/Children (2)	80,000	80,000	—
5026-Admin. Assists (2)	36,000	36,000	—
5021-Maint./Custodial (2)	38,000	38,000	—
	279,000	279,000	—
5040-Payroll Taxes, Benefits			
5045-Payroll Taxes	70,000	70,000	—
5050-Health Insurance	45,000	45,000	—
5080-Workers Comp.	3,000	3,000	—
	118,000	118,000	—
5300-Family Ministries			
5310-Seminars	300	1,500	(1,200)
5315-Seminars, Income	1,300	(1,200)	2,500
5320-Curriculum	400	600	(200)
	2,000	900	1,100
5400-Women's Ministries			
5401-Income (Retreat)	(8,950)	(9,300)	(350)
5415-MOPS	1,875	2,000	(125)
5330-Women's Outreach	1,484	1,150	334
5440-Women's Retreat	8,851	9,000	(149)
	4,669	4,200	(231)
5500-Adults			
5501-Adult Sunday School	1,011	1,000	11
5510-Adult Growth Groups	1,328	1,000	328
5530-Fundamentals of Faith	175	225	(50)
5535-Senior Ministry	200	300	(100)
	2,714	2,525	189
Total Expense	389,858	71,515	16,808
TOTAL SURPLUS/LOSS	$2,279	$2,485	($206)

Heavenly Valley Community Church Balance Sheet
FYE 20__

ASSETS	31-Dec-00
Current Assets	
Checking/Savings	
Cash-Checking Account	$ 5,974
Fidelity Investments	125,000
Restricted-Building Fund	225,000
Total	355,974
Land, Buildings, and Equipment	
Land	970,000
Buildings	1,750,000
Equipment	25,000
	2,745,000
Less accumulated depreciation	(125,000)
Total	2,620,000
Other Assets	
Gift property held for sale (automobile)	15,000
Petty cash	300
Total Other Assets	15,300
TOTAL ASSETS	$2,991,274
LIABILITIES AND NET ASSETS	
Current Liabilities	
Accounts Payable	$ 1,300
Current maturities of long-term debt	22,000
Payroll Taxes Due	2,706
Current Liabilities	26,006
Long-Term Debt Less Current Maturities	975,000
Total Liabilities	$1,001,006
Net Assets	
Temporary Restricted:	
Scholarship Fund	20,000
Building Fund	225,000
	245,000
Unrestricted:	
Net investment in property and equipment	1,745,268
Total Net Assets	1,990,268
Total Liabilities and Net Assets	$2,991,274

How Much and How Little?

OK, with that brief accounting lesson behind us, how does this relate to the question of transparency? The members of your congregation need to be assured the money they gave to a specific project or program was either used correctly or that any surplus or unused funds are still available and not comingled with other funds. So once again, in the spirit of clarity, the practical value of the balance sheet is it should show the amount of funds precisely in what is called Semi Restricted Funds. To illustrate, let's say the church announced it was going to start to raise funds for a new building. And after one year, $225,000 was received. How would you assure people where that money was, and how would you declare to the donors it wasn't being commingled with other income and even lost? The answer is it would appear on the balance sheet in a restricted or protected account. Notice on the balance sheet sample where the $225,000 is shown. It's in two places. First, it is an asset because it's money collected and sitting in a bank account. But it is also a liability because it has an obligation placed on it. That is, it was received with a purpose and stated intention: to build a building. Thus, it is "owed" to something and thus a liability. If any of those funds were spent, that amount would be reduced. (At the risk of confusing you, I'll just point out that the income and expenses associated with the building fund would also appear in the profit and loss statement, but let's just leave it at that!)

These two financial reports are usually sufficient for those individuals who are responsible for the oversight of the church's finances and be in a position to make clear, informed decisions. There are other more detailed and sophisticated reports that could be produced; but making those available would depend on the size of the church, the level of authority of the reviewing individual, and, in some cases, the ability of those reading the reports to interpret them properly. People may be dazzled with complicated financial reports, but if they can't understand them, why bother?

And this brings us down to the basic question posed at the beginning of this chapter. Who should be receiving financial reports? How detailed should they be? Providing detailed financial statements to congregations can often cause more problems than necessary to understand the basic financial condition of churches.

Here's the point for you to understand. When the leadership of a church asks the congregation to give money to support the needs of the church, people have a right to be assured that the funds are being handled properly. It all boils down to an issue of trust. Each church experiences a level of trust based on a track record of the finance people. No matter whether the church is elder rule or congregation rule, certain persons are entrusted with the handling of the funds; and it is at this point where people are comfortable with the way finances are handled, or they are suspicious.

From my experience, reports are provided to specific levels of leadership and the congregation as a whole based on a need to know. If the financial reporting over the years has been done in a professional manner and the people charged with the oversight have demonstrated integrity and credibility, then the financial reports can be pegged to the need-to-know level. You can tell when there is a perception of mistrust when larger numbers of people ask for greater detail in the reporting process. Yes, there will be those holdouts in the congregation who want a line-by-line budget report; but generally, not always, they can be dealt with privately, addressing their concerns in a less confrontational environment.

To sum up, I'd suggest producing a P&L and balance sheet for the church treasurer; and if there is a finance committee, they should have one too. If there are issues or irregularities, every attempt should be made to address and correct those at that level.

As far a reporting to the congregation, well, that all depends! How's that for dodging an issue? But in reality, it does all depend. It depends, as I said before, on the history of reporting the church finances, the credibility of the leaders, and the level of comfort expressed by the people in the congregation.

Today, there are any number of creative ways to produce reports suitable for a congregation's review and approval if required. There are computer programs you can buy right off the shelf of an office supply store that will produce graphic representations and illustrations of financial reports in clear, easily understood formats such as pie charts, line and bar graphs, and the other display methods. A newly developed and creative presentation format is called a Dashboard, which organizes information so that it's easy to read and interpret. Information is presented visually through graphics: charts, gauges, maps, and tables. They are very innovative and now available for church applications.

There is one specific area of reporting, however, that does present challenges in some churches—that is, reporting the pastor's salary. And again, we are faced with that church culture tradition. There are churches that publish their financial information in detailed form, showing each pastor's salary as a line item. Others group staff salaries as one lump sum number. There are those who place the salaries within the individual ministries, such as youth or worship ministry. Then there are reports that show compensation under comprehensive headings such as "Program" and "General and Administration."

I realize there are those people in a congregation who feel it is their right to know how every penny is spent. Some will have a desire for this information for all the wrong reasons: comparison, jealousy, or other motives. But as one pastor told me, "If someone had a request for more detailed information such as the pastor's salary, I would entertain their request and make a decision on that on a case-by-case basis. If their heart was right and they needed to know, I would consider that. If I sense they are just a problem person, I wouldn't do any more, and I'd tell them why." Another pastor said, "Money will always be a point of contention. But integrity, honesty, and openness dispels all accusations and complaints."

In the final analysis, the congregation needs to trust their board of directors to deal with the finances in a "representative type of government." This is preferable than having the whole congregation getting involved because they lack enough information to judge properly. Things can be misinterpreted because people form opinions based on their own circumstances or experiences without having contextual or comprehensive information.

Those that need to know should be informed. The rest should simply trust their leaders and move on to those matters that impact the kingdom of God.

Spending

Who's in Charge Here?

How the church's money is spent can present some very complex and sometimes thorny challenges. The pressure point here is one of control. That is, who has the right to spend and keep an eye on the flow of funds in and out of the church?

It's been said that the more the board controls the spending, the less a ministry can respond to needs. Nimbleness and flexibility are dampened when the board needs to approve all expenditures. On the other hand, the more freedom is granted to ministries, the more difficult it becomes to monitor exactly what is taking place as far as cash flow is concerned and adhering to the goal of staying within approved budgets.

There are many examples that illustrate the challenges of this question. For instance:

- The church buys a new video camera. Which ministry is to be charged with the expense even though everyone wants to use it?
- There is a "mystery" charge for $175.45 at the Christian bookstore. Who bought this material, and was it for Sunday school or youth ministry?
- The women's ministry just concluded a retreat, and the leaders are turning in request for reimbursement. But where are the receipts?
- Our printing costs are running twice as much as we budgeted for. Who is going to pay for these additional expenses?

These issues can appear even though an annual budget was carefully crafted six months ago and the board, staff, and congregation all approved it. Policies and procedures have been put in place; there is even a P&P (policies and procedures) handbook that was prepared by a church member who is an astute businessman.

Often, in smaller churches, laypeople make purchases without seeking approval from a board in advance. Or the process of getting a signed purchase order from the church treasure can be difficult, time-consuming, or "Sorry, he's on vacation this week!"

Every church has to determine what the best method is for them to accurately watch their expenses. Much depends on the size of the church. Actually, the larger churches tend to have fewer problems because a staff person, usually a church business administrator, is assigned to manage to church finances; and hopefully, that person has the authority to approve or disapprove expenditures based on approved policies and procedures. Unfortunately, this can place the business manager in a difficult position because the church is made up of both paid staff and church members who donate money to the church. There are many vested interests or, as is the common phrase, stakeholders.

There are two major issues at play here: First, who has the authority to say yes or no, to approve or disapprove spending? Second, how much discretion should ministry department heads have over their budgets? Do they have to spend funds exactly as budgeted for specific line items, or can they move funds around within their budgets as needs arise or circumstances change?

It Starts at the Top

The solution to these two questions is embodied in the established policies and procedures of the church as set forth by the ruling body. A P&P handbook is not that difficult to create. Today, with the advent of computerized software, templates that can be reproduced by a church to fit their specific needs are readily available. A simple format can be found in my book *Business Management in the Local Church* (Moody Press, 1996). There are other software programs available through various companies. An excellent clearing house for these resources is Ministry Business Services (*www.mbsinc.com*).

But more to the point—and here is where it can get tricky—within the written and approved polices, there should be a clear identification of responsibilities. An appointed individual or a group must, for the sake of efficiency, decide the most appropriate process for disbursing church funds. I prefer a layered approach of assigning these responsibilities. First, it begins with the ruling board of the church. They have the final say when it comes to approving the budget or making major decisions regarding income and spending.

Second, I'd assign the task of monitoring the expenses to the church treasurer if the church is small or, if affordable, a church business administration or business manager. Again, the original policies and procedures handbook will make it clear that this person will have the authority to approve purchases that are unusual or outside of budgeted guidelines.

The final level would be the individual responsible for the area of ministry. It may be a paid staff person, a lay leader, or a combination of both. This in most cases will eliminate the fuzziness of who has the authority to spend funds allocated to a specific ministry. This entitles this person to "own" their own budgets yet be accountable.

By designing a system that has this three-tiered structure, many of the pressure points connected with spending money can be lessened. For instance, if the youth leader sees an opportunity to spend money on an outreach project outside of his budget, he doesn't have to go to the pastor of the church to gain approval. He can use the "chain of command," so to speak, to gain permission from either his lay counterpart or, the next level up, the business manager or treasurer. It's important that more than one person is kept in the loop when making purchases out of the budgeted line items. Again, if the women's ministry leader wants to buy a new DVD for a Bible study, she shouldn't have to contact the church office first. She should have a contact person available who has the authority to approve the expense.

Ideally, as an example, the youth pastor is given the responsibility for the youth budget. So when a senior high Bible study leader wants to buy study guides for the book of Romans, he would go to the youth pastor to determine where the funds would come from within the youth ministry budget. If any purchase is outside the youth ministry budget, then the request moves up the line to the next person in authority.

This eliminates the need for people to seek permission from the board of directors or the senior pastor to make purchases for every item. Getting permission to buy food for a memorial service should not require board approval. This expense would be a line item in a specific department budget overseen by an appointed person. The goal here is to keep the process uncomplicated, simple, and with a minimum of bureaucracy and red tape!

Does this always work smoothly? No, because not every situation is the same or cookie-cutter-like in its circumstances. But a multilayered approach makes it easier to manage the financial dealings of the church and specific ministries. However, I have been around long enough to know that not every church board is comfortable with this approach. In some cases, it means relinquishing control over spending and trusting others to manage their own department's finances. There is an argument that a board loses its authority to monitor activities if it stops requiring ministries to report changes in their budgeted spending. The issue of a board following a "governing" versus a "managing" model and practice was discussed earlier in this book. The point is, how much control is too much or too little?

Then there are those who believe that as long as a department or ministry stays within their overall budgeted amount, they should be free to make changes as they feel necessary. It's like with our own personal funds; we must live within our means—no credit cards to fall back on or overdraft protection!

Exceptions to the Rule

Unforeseen expenses or opportunities will come up—you can count on them. Equipment breaks down, a roof can spring a leak, and the annual pastor's conference is rescheduled and is one thousand miles away with an increase cost over the last two years' conferences. These can be nonbudgeted items or present themselves as large unaccounted-for costs. The ruling board would then decide what, if any, adjustments to the overall budget should be made. It's always a good idea to include a line item for "contingencies" in a budget. But this fund needs to be used sparingly, or else it becomes a meaningless "slush fund" over time. The safest policy would be if the expense is not in the budget, it needs to gain approval from the appropriate level, especially if it's a major expense. Those exceptions can become the rule if everyone isn't on board with these "emergency" needs.

It should be added that once an exception is granted, the budget should not be changed to reflect that overage unless this is a true *recurring* expense or an oversight. It is advisable to leave the budget figures the same and then address this need when the budget comes up for consideration the next year. It can then be decided if this is going to be a regular cost or it was in fact an exception to the rule.

This all comes down to the level of trust the ruling board places in the people charged with the oversight of their ministry's finances. Often, this is trial and error process; but in the long run, I believe this three-level approach is best for all concerned and will greatly reduce the pressure points of spending.

DESIGNATED GIVING

Giving with Strings Attached

A note found in the offering plate read, "The enclosed check for $500 is to go toward the purchase of a new church organ." Also, Mr. Green, a regular giver, is now requesting that his weekly contribution be sent to feed hungry children in Uganda. In addition, Joe Johnson, the youth pastor, received a gift of $100 from an anonymous donor: "In appreciation for all you've done to help my daughter get her life back on track."

All these gifts are certainly appreciated, but what should church leaders do if they don't need a new organ or know of a way to get money to needy Ugandan children? And maybe the youth pastor just got a raise. The church doesn't want to return the gifts, yet donors have placed certain conditions on the way church leaders should spend them.

Donations given to the church with specific instructions for their use, commonly known as designated gifts, cannot quietly be added to the general fund and spent for current needs. Both the Internal Revenue Service and the donor have a legal and moral right to know exactly how a designated gift is spent. Gifts designated for missions projects, "love offerings" for speakers, donations to meet financial needs of church members, and funds given to finance concerts, musicals, films, radio programs, and scholarships for camps and schools must be carefully accounted for.

Perhaps you like to earmark your giving so that you have control over where it is spent. But place yourself in the position of the church treasurer, who with each designated gift faces a bittersweet dilemma: how could he deal with the gift in a way that is agreeable to the donor, consistent with the overall mission, (specifically the purposes of the church,) and in keeping with guidelines of the IRS and the principles of wise stewardship?

The proper handling of designated gifts could present a pressure point for the treasurer. How? Because he could be challenged with questions that involve ethical and legal accounting issues.

The Internal Revenue Service makes it clear what can and cannot be considered a tax-deductible contribution. And in the case of designated gifts, it states there are some contributions you cannot deduct. You cannot deduct as a charitable contribution a contribution to a specific individual, a contribution to a nonqualified organization, the part of a contribution from which you receive or expect to receive a benefit, the value of your time or services, and your personal expenses.[1]

The wise treasurer asks two sets of questions:

1. Is the direction of this gift in line with the priorities of our church? If not, should we reevaluate our priorities in order to pursue the objective of the giver?

2. If we return the gift, what effect will our refusal have on the donor? How can we best handle our refusal?

If the gift is to an individual on the church staff, two additional concerns need to be addressed.

One has to do with fairness to other church employees. Staff members in positions of high visibility tend to receive special gifts. They are the ones who receive a free week at a member's condo in the mountains, gift baskets at Christmas, and, in the case of our example, a "love gift" in the form of money. But the men and women working in support roles will have needs just as great—and possibly, they are even greater, depending on their family situation. Is the church prepared to offer them matching gifts? And if so, where does it end?

The second concern is that the donor needs to know that a gift designated to an individual is not tax deductible. The law states, "If contributions . . . are earmarked by a donor for a particular individual, they are treated, in effect, as being gifts to the designated individual and are not deductible."[2] The treasurer may determine that a designated gift cannot be utilized in the way it was intended. As painful as it may be, he must openly and honestly talk to the person offering the gift, tactfully encouraging him to continue in his spirit of generosity by helping the church leaders meet the priorities and goals of the church.

Often, it is helpful to get out ahead of the curve on matters that can be challenging, and this is just one case in point. It needs to be understood by both the leadership of the church and its members that all statements made by the church in its stewardship appeals concerning the use of contributions must absolutely be honored. What is communicated by the church will shape the donor's intent through the donor's instructions with their gift. If a donor makes a gift in response to a specific appeal, then that constitutes both the donor's intent and the church's duty to apply the gift "as advertised."

For example, if an appeal is made for funds for a special project, let's say a short-term mission venture, then any response to the appeal must be restricted to that project.

Who may restrict a gift? Only donors can restrict a gift. Furthermore, gifts from an accounting standpoint are either temporary or permanent, depending on the specific wording of the funds appeal. This should be made clear from the outset—that is, make it plain for how long and how much funding will be needed for a specific project.

There are two common examples of how this ruling is to be applied. For instance, what is the proper way to contribute to a specific mission trip in order to raise support for individuals? Is it OK for supporters to write the name of the mission's trip as well as the name of a specific individual who will be a part of that mission's project? The solution and remedy would be to establish an individual fund for the individual, but unfortunately, it wouldn't be considered a tax-deductible gift. The reason is because this is what's called a pass-through gift, and the IRS does not permit this type of contribution. That rule especially applies when the contributor is also going on the trip. In other words, a gift given for their personal support is not tax deductible. (More on this specific issue in the next chapter.)

The understanding and application of the law is more than a matter of one's own opinion or interpretation. In 1990, the Supreme Court ruled in *Davis v. United States*[3] for the first time on the issue of whether payments made "to or for the use of" a qualified organization were deductible as charitable contributions. The taxpayers, whom were members of the Church of Jesus Christ of Latter-Day Saints (church), claimed such deductions for funds transferred to their sons while they were serving as full-time unpaid missionaries for the church. The church requested payments, set the amounts, and through written guidelines instructed that they were to be used exclusively for missionary work. In accordance with the guidelines, their sons used the money primarily to pay rent, food, and transportation, as well as for personal needs while on their missions. The Supreme Court denied deductibility. It doesn't get any clearer than that!

Another issue that comes up often is the tax deductibility of payments to private church schools for tuition. Again, there cannot be a connection between the parent, relative, or friend of the student with the payment of the tuition. Yes, the school can have a scholarship fund; but it must be available to other qualified students, and again, the donor can't specify a certain student.

An indication of an earmarked donation is when someone says they want to "run it through the ministry" or "pass this gift onto through the church." This is why churches should be very careful and understand what constitutes a "conduit gift" and what the terminology as a pass through gift even sounds like. While the donor's intentions may be genuine, loving, and sincere, the basic difficulty is their desire for control of how the money is to be spent.

The problem is many organizations are lax in their oversight of this area, and they don't want to offend donors. But again, the law is clear on what can and cannot be considered a tax-deductible gift.

Indeed, a deeper issue is at stake than the legal mechanics of handling designated gifts. The biblical concept of church leadership authority may be threatened by designated giving. Acts 4:35 sets forth a rather subtle yet profound practice. New Testament believers were truly committed to meeting the needs of others; but instead of giving gifts directly to certain individuals or special projects, they would lay their gifts, in a manner of speaking, "at the apostles' feet, and they would be distributed to each as they had need."

Again, there is a biblical component to this issue determining how funds are to be spent. The New Testament apostles were godly men with a proven track record of being good stewards. They were in a position to know the needs and requirements of the local body. As the God-ordained leaders of the body, they determined where and how resources were to be spent. It wasn't a case of a small group of powerful men trying to call all the shots. They were honest, trustworthy, and properly motivated men who knew where and how to get the job done. And people confidently submitted to their leadership. The modern-day application of that first-century principle is threefold:

First, the responsibility of church finances should be placed in the hands of trusted, duly appointed leaders. Biblical church leadership is not by majority rule. Decisions—financial and otherwise—should be made according to the wisdom of godly leaders who are charged with the responsibility of overseeing the entire organization.

Second, establish an annual budget that provides funds for all church ministries—a "unified budget." Here, different ministries are kept separate for internal bookkeeping purposes. The fund for the new electronic keyboard, the debt reduction fund, the camp scholarship fund, and the myriad of other special-emphasis areas that tend to encourage designated giving can be allowed for on a limited basis in this way. If the church leaders recognize a major specific area of need, they bring that need before the congregation of the church to then request designated gifts.

Finally, establish a written policy limiting the solicitation and receiving of gifts for designated nonbudgeted purposes. A suggested policy might read something like this:

> Contributions will not be received that are designated for organizations or individuals not recognized by the Internal Revenue Service as tax-exempt.

> Contributions can be designated for particular purposes, programs, or projects of the church itself that have been duly authorized in advance as part of the religious activity of the board of elders (or your particular ruling body). Expenditures of such

contributions for the purposes designated will be entirely within
the discretion of the church or its appropriate internal body.

If the church cannot find a way to utilize such contributions
within its own purposes and the donor's designation, it will
return the donation to the donor with an explanation of the
problem.

The church will determine the best means of carrying out its
purposes with such contributions. If an outside agency is utilized,
the church will continue to exercise expenditure accountability
to make sure that its funds are applied to its purpose by any
contractor, agent, or grantee.

In the final analysis, the practice of designated giving not only drains
away from the church's financial base, but also sets up a framework in
which people can in fact "vote" with their checkbooks. In some situations,
the church may be struggling just to pay the light bill or minister's salary. A
new stained-glass window simply may not be one of the pressing priorities.
But the decision should be made by the church's spiritual leaders, not
the people who have the most money.

Whether you agree or disagree with this approach, nevertheless, the
practice of giving with strings attached can become a pressure point if
not dealt with in a fair but legal manner.

1. Internal Revenue Service, Publication 526
2. Internal Revenue Service, Ruling 62-113 (1962)
3. Davis v United States, 495 U.S. 472 (1990)

Short-Term Mission Projects

Dos and Don'ts

Over the last few years, many churches have expanded their missions and outreach ministries to include short-term mission (STM) programs. While many of these programs and people involved have been criticized as being what's been termed "vacationaries," there are nevertheless tax implications that can easily become *pressure points* if not dealt with correctly. Violations could be committed without a basic knowledge of what is and what is not considered a tax-deductible donation in support of these programs. The IRS has made it clear what is acceptable in regard to fund-raising for STM programs.

First, it should be understood that donations for the benefit of an individual are not deductible—period. If folks donate to their church or even a Christian school on behalf of a specific individual, it is not deductible. The concept of "full control and discretion" was discussed in the previous chapter, and the same principle applies in the case of STMs. The donor must understand and agree that the church will decide how to spend those funds within the STM framework. That means the funds may not go to support a specific person, but the program as a whole.

On the other hand, STM program expenses that are paid by the individual for their own expenses are deductible. It should be noted, however, that if expenses are incurred for what could only be considered a tour, such as a Holy Land Tour or a Christian cruise to Mediterranean New Testament sites, are not deductible.

So here are some suggestions and rules relating to tax deductions for short-term mission trips?

- The overall purpose of the trip must adhere to your church's mission. To organize a trip to the Holy Land as a tourist while it may be educational is not considered a missionary activity. However, if the trip is to support the efforts of a church in Jerusalem and their programs directly, that is acceptable. This is another one of those cases where you should consult with a tax professional as part of the planning stages of the STM.

- There needs to be church oversight of the trip. An itinerary and planned activities that are in direct relationship to missionary work must be spelled out in advance. What do you intend to accomplish on the trip?

- The church needs to have a preplanned budget that spells out in as much detail as possible the costs of the trip. They are to include travel, food, lodging, and miscellaneous expenses. If a per diem for expenses is to be provided, seek advice from a tax professional first to determine what is allowable. These expenses and specific provisions must be consistent with tax law.

- If church staff members or other participants are being compensated, the amounts should be reasonable and objective. If a compensated individual is raising their own support, the amount they raised cannot be an unreasonable amount.

- Any discussions with participants regarding their donations to the STM should emphasize that raising a certain amount of money is not a condition of their involvement. Their fund-raising is to help the church STM cover the costs and not their "price of admission." This is a very important point, and they must fully understand this position before they begin to raise funds.

- There should be some advance training for the STM. Individuals need to know what is expected of them, how to act in foreign environments, and what health resources are available (if any!)—within reason, everything that can be anticipated.

- Finally, it's always a good idea to have the participants report back to the church's oversight body and even the congregation once the STM participants have returned. A full accounting of the expenses and funds disbursed connected with the project should be fully reported.

Short-term mission projects can be an important part of encouraging and advancing the outreach of a local church. Those participating in these projects are often asked to raise their own support, which is an effective way to get people to be involved in missions. The key once again is the church must establish the objectives of the trip beforehand; they must maintain control of the activities involved, and the church must demonstrate that it has control over the use of the funds raised for the project. This way, the contributions will be tax deductible to donors.

The following are frequently asked questions relating to tax issues connected with short-term missions.

Short-Term Mission Trips: Frequently Asked Questions*

Are gifts for short-term mission trips deductible as charitable gifts?

Generally, yes, but it depends on the facts and circumstances. To be tax deductible, gifts to support a trip participant, especially gifts from the trip participant, must be subject to the discretion and control of the sponsoring church; the trip must be for legitimate mission purposes, and the trip participants must fulfill those purposes

Are funds given to a church deductible when the gifts are intended for participants in a specific trip and the participants are minors?

It depends. The minor must actually provide services to carry out the tax-exempt purposes of the trip. The age of the minor and minor's development may be important factors in determining the minor's capability of providing services to the church.

Is it appropriate for a donor to indicate a preference or express a desire that a gift be used to fund the trip of a particular participant, even if the donor is the trip participant or a relative?

If only a preference is made for the gift to be used to fund the expenses of a particular participant and refunds are not given to prospective participants who are not able to go on the trip, gifts are generally deductible if the trip is sponsored or approved by the church; the trip is consistent with the tax-exempt purposes of the church, and there is no significant element of personal pleasure, recreation, or vacation.

Can short-term mission trip participants pay part or all of the trip expenses out of their pocket, with no financial involvement of the sponsoring church?

Yes, if the trip is sponsored or approved by the church, the trip is consistent with the tax-exempt purposes of the church and there is no significant element of personal pleasure, recreation, or vacation. If the trip meets these thresholds, the church should provide a written acknowledgment to the trip participant for out-of-pocket expenses.

Is it appropriate for a church to sponsor and fund a short-term mission trip with funds in the church's budget or with funds raised for a short-term mission trip project (its donors did not indicate an interest in supporting any particular participant)?

Yes, if the purposes of the trip are consistent with the tax-exempt purposes of the church and there is no significant element of personal pleasure, recreation, or vacation with respect to the participants.

Should funds ever be refunded to donors when a potential short-term mission trip participant does not go on the trip and gifts have been preferenced for the individual not going on the trip?

Generally no. Sponsoring churches should have a policy prohibiting refunds of gifts relating to short-term mission trips. Refunding a mission trip gift is evidence of the lack of the necessary discretion and control by the sponsoring church over gifts, thereby placing the tax deductibility of the gifts at risk.

*Source: Evangelical Council for Financial Accountability (ECFA)

ECFA is an accreditation agency dedicated to helping Christian ministries earn the public's trust through adherence to **Seven Standards of Responsible Stewardship**. Founded in 1979, ECFA provides accreditation to leading Christian nonprofit organizations that faithfully demonstrate compliance with established standards for financial accountability, fund-raising, and board governance. Members include Christian ministries, denominations, churches, educational institutions, and other tax-exempt 501 (c) (3) organizations. Collectively, these organizations represent more than $18 billion in annual revenue.

Budgeting and Planning

Ministry within Boundaries

I have been asked, "So who needs a budget? This is a ministry, not a business. Let's just spend money as the Lord provides. If God is in it, He will supply!" One pastor told me, "Budgets limit God!" Is he right? Do budgets limit the work of the Holy Spirit in a church?

The reality of the issue is that for a church to be successful in managing its financial resources, budgets are an absolute necessity. Many in leadership consider them a necessary evil. They aren't looked upon favorably, and the only people who enjoy the process are the "bean counter" types. This perception can be a major pressure point and a challenge to the vitality of a local church and, in some extreme cases, to its very existence.

Budgeting Defined

In planning and budgeting, the church will be saying something significant. It will be making a statement to itself and to its community—and ultimately to God, who raised up and sustains the church. Planning and budgeting impact the church's witness and the "story" it seeks to tell.

Webster defines a budget as "an estimate of future financial income and outgo." That's it! As cold and sterile as that may sound, the leadership of the church should still look *beyond* the "income and outgo" aspects of budgeting.

Scripture gives us a more wide-ranging definition. "Is there anyone here who, planning to build a new house, doesn't first sit down and figure the cost so you'll know if you can complete it? If you only get the foundation laid and then run out of money, you're going to look pretty foolish. Everyone passing by will poke fun at you: 'He started something he couldn't finish'" (Luke 14:28-30, the Message).

It is important to change the paradigm of thinking about budgets. They don't dictate what is done. Instead, they are supposed to conform to the vision and plan of the church's leadership. The budget should enhance what the church wants to be and do under God's leading. Simply stated, plan carefully first—and then budget. Budgets are the church's plans put to numbers with dollar signs! Perhaps it would be best to start by asking, "What does the budget reveal about the church's ministry priorities?" Often, the budget is a very good indication of where the leadership of the church places its value.

Budget Development

A ministry leader once told me, "We prepare a budget every year and then practically abandon it after six months because things change so much." This is a very common problem. There are three essentials elements needed to insure an effective church budget:

1. Good Participation.

It is vital that a budget process begins not with how much money a church has or can expect to have, but with the needs it wants to meet. Budgeting in an evangelical organization should be "ministry driven." It begins with a select group of board members and includes the top church staff. The vision for the ministry comes from the leadership as God guides them. Paid staff members work with lay leaders to derive a plan for ministry, which results in a budget proposal to the church's board.

There is a popular term in use today that relates to a person's involvement in a ministry. They are called stakeholders. Those individuals, who will have the responsibility to manage their specific ministry budget, should have a say in how it is funded. Participation on the part of the church leaders will usually produce a "buying in" process and ensure better cooperation and compliance.

2. Good Numbers

Looking Back
Past income patterns are important in helping you determine whether you can afford to fund what you believe is needed. This

information can often demonstrate past trends relating to spending, expenses, and costs connected with ministry thrusts (i.e., short-term mission trips, significant building maintenance or upgrades, etc.). For instance, in the area of giving, how much have contributions increased over the last three years? Can you expect this trend to continue? Why? The leaders need to do their homework to arrive at good, usable numbers. This information can be retrieved from past financial statements, bankbooks, ledgers, and so forth. It is helpful, therefore, to develop a simple profile of past performance.

Looking Ahead

Since budgets are customarily designed to accommodate a twelve-month period, long-range plans must be accounted for in this process as well.

It is advisable to form a budget committee that is also forward thinking. One that looks years ahead—one to three years—is important. Anticipated numerical growth should be considered in the event that additional or expanded facilities are needed.

The local economy should be considered as well. Local banks often produce an annual economic outlook report. These may be "educated guesses," but a guess by an educated, informed person is better than blindly going forward without a contingency or a fall-back plan.

It is at this point where future pressure points can be avoided by asking specific questions that could easily impact the budget projections. For instance:

- Are there any income-producing contracts that may expire or renew and at what levels?
- How likely is the church congregation giving going to increase, or will there be revenue coming in from planned special events?
- What are your earned income trends from reserve accounts? For instance, interest rates from certificates of deposit, money market, or mutual funds?
- How does your personnel policy impact your future budget? That is, do you offer benefits that kick in after an employee has passed a probationary period (i.e., three months or six months or even five years for long-term staff members)?

- Are future annual raises being considered and on what basis? If it's a percentage of the base salary, then that base will continue to expand each year—something to take into consideration, by the way, when offerings by percentage don't rise across the board.
- What increases are built into any leases for property, building or equipment?
- Have known or announced rate increases scheduled for utilities, postage, or other services been considered?

3. Good Fit

The budget needs to be achievable. I have actually seen churches increase their budgets in the face of steadily declining income because to do otherwise would demonstrate a lack of faith in God's provision. They were more concerned with what people would think instead of facing the reality of the way things actually were. Furthermore, there are those who would argue that people need to be "stretched," to "step out on faith," to be challenged. However, church leaders need to keep in mind that there is a fine line between faith and presumption. Many ministries "write checks" and then expect God to "cash" them. To undertake a project that will require a 15 percent increase in giving over the next year, when, in fact, the giving has only been increasing 6 percent over the last three years could be a huge mistake.

A budget must fit the ability of the congregation to make donations. Without a question, there certainly is a place for faith when it comes to giving. However, the faith challenge needs to be realistic and within the capability of the donors to meet the need. That is why looking back at past performance and then looking ahead with an understanding of the basic economic factors that affect giving will go a long way toward producing a budget that will be a good fit for the church.

Production Process

Many of you may be familiar with the KISS principle—the polite spelled-out version of which is "*keep it simple, saint.*" Well, when it comes to budgeting, the best course of action is to keep the process of producing a budget as simple as possible. No matter the size of your church, the basic format scarcely changes.

A budget generally follows a format that is inclusive of all sources of revenue and expenses. Simply illustrated, a budget would include the following:

Anatomy of a Basic Budget
INCOME

Revenue: Earned Income
      Product sales (books, Bibles, CDs, DVDs, misc.)
      Interest from reserve investments
      Special events
      Camps and retreats

Revenue: Contributed Income
      Donations (tithes and offerings)
      Special events (net income)
      Camps and retreats (net income)

      Subtotal
      TOTAL INCOME

EXPENSES
Personnel expenses
      Salaries
      Benefits @ _% of salaries
      Independent contractors
      Subtotal personnel

Nonpersonnel expenses
      Rent/mortgage
      Administrative/finance
      Utilities
      Building and grounds
      Information technology
      Insurance
      Office supplies
      Program/ministry
      Missions/outreach
      Printing
      Subtotal nonpersonnel
      TOTAL EXPENSES
      Balance (the difference between total income and total expenses)

There are two common budget formats used in ministries: the line-item budget and the ministry-based budget. For our purposes, we will use both methods. That is, we will recommend a ministry-based budget that contains line items.

First Step: Programs and Church Departments

In the first step, the entire church structure is broken down into programs or departments (i.e., administration, worship/music, youth/children's ministry, outreach/missions, etc.). Each program or department is assigned either a staff person (if the church is large) or a lay leader (if the church is small). This individual is responsible for determining needs, projecting income (if appropriate, such as fees for events, training sessions, etc.), and forming the expense portion of the budget.

Second Step: Line Items

Each department should have "line items" assigned to the revenue and expense portion of the budget. This means that every conceivable type of expense should have a category and be placed in the budget. For example, Christian education (CE) could have a separate line entry labeled "Training Materials" for items such a training manuals, brochures, etc. Then if several items are similar, they can be grouped together under single line items. Using the CE example again, you might place "Training Materials" in with "Equipment" (such as a new DVD player) and title them both as "Teaching Aids" or "Material and Equipment." If the church is quite small, simply put all CE expenses under one heading. With the advent of inexpensive off-the-shelf accounting software, having line items is actually quite simple to manage.

The line-item method allows you the freedom to be as detailed as you choose. You can plan for and track any segment of the church budget you desire. Words of caution though: don't get too general and lump everything together into as few categories as possible. That only defeats the purpose of planning and control.

Many of the expenses of the church are assigned to what is often referred to as "General and Administrative" (or G&A). The leadership should decide, for instance, if they want the salaries of each staff person to appear within their own program department or to have them assigned to a G&A category. Other expenses such as postage, printing, paid employee benefits, and other general expenses need to be assigned somewhere. This tends to be based on the philosophy of the church. That is, do the leaders want to know the exact cost of a ministry, which includes staff, and certain overhead costs? Or do they wish to have these expenses posted in a separate category?

The goal here is to be sure that every expected expense is placed into a department line item. This will prevent funds or expenses from "falling through the cracks."

Third Step: Revenue and Expenses

If it is anticipated that there will be fees and charges for a program or event, list them as both revenue and expense. This is important, but it can be a source of confusion. That is, when an event is planned and a fee charged, the income should match the expense unless it is understood in advance that there is a going to be a shortfall. Of course, unforeseen problems can arise; but if this happens, often within a specific program, leaders should address it.

Fourth Step: Chart of Accounts

Line item numbers and labels are now to be assigned to the dollar amount. These form what is referred to as a chart of accounts. Each line item is an "account."

Sample Format: Small Church

A smaller church may want to follow a simple, more general format. The sample at the end of the chapter shows a basic budget that can be expanded (by adding more line items) or kept shorter (by grouping all similar line items into one line item). For example, a smaller church would have one line item for salaries and expenses instead of breaking this category out by department, as is the case in a larger church. This example is only an aid, and you should make changes where they are appropriate.

Although the first time you prepare a budget using these methods may require a lot of effort, the next time will be much simpler. Even though using this method—a combination line-item and program-item budget could result in more line-items entries that you had in past budgets—it will still be easier to track income and expenses with this approach.

Sample Format: Large Church

Due to the size, complexity, and the amount of money flowing through a large church's financial books, a more detailed budget format is needed. See the example at the end of the chapter.

Presentation

Once the budget is approved (and depending on how it is presented to the board), the form in which the budget is presented is important. Many churches simply publish pages with numbers and line items. For a lot of people, this is difficult to understand. Board members generally would like the budget presentation to be simple. They would like to know the following:

- What was our income last year?
- What was last year's budget?
- Did we accomplish the projections or miss them? By how much?
- What is the projected income for the new year?
- What is the new expense budget?
- What are the major categories?
- Do the leaders expect us to achieve our goal?

Today's computer technology allows any financial report to be interesting and easy to understand. In fact, financial information can be presented in a way that inspires people. Here are some suggestions:

Make the reports live and breathe. If the budget is presented to the board, why not ask those involved in the specific programs to represent those line items and give reports or stories that demonstrate the successes of the past year. I have seen a budget presentation consist of people from each of the church's major programs who gave an "annual report" complete with PowerPoint presentations, photographs, and graphs. They definitely put faces on the finances!

Another presentation started with the senior pastor giving a report card on the accomplishments of the church over the last twelve months, followed by his vision for the next year. He then explained how the ministry plans were going to be funded, program by program in broad strokes.

In some instances, those who prepared the budget may want to show the board of directors how the income and expenses compare with the previous year yet offer a reasonable amount of detail. A summarized format would be used, and the various ministries would be shown with lump sum amounts for their transactions compared with the amounts budgeted, and then a difference or variance will be shown.

As an example of how financial facts can be illustrated in a visual presentation, the following graph shows the cumulative (or running) totals through the past year and how they compare with each other.

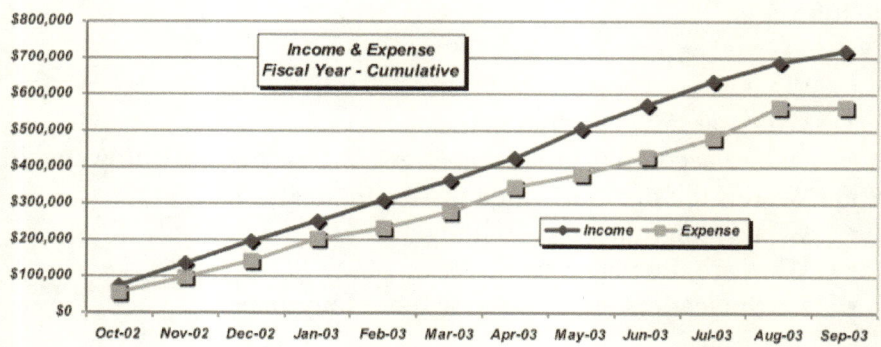

The visual pie chart format shown below would demonstrate how the projected expenses would be allocated over the next fiscal year.

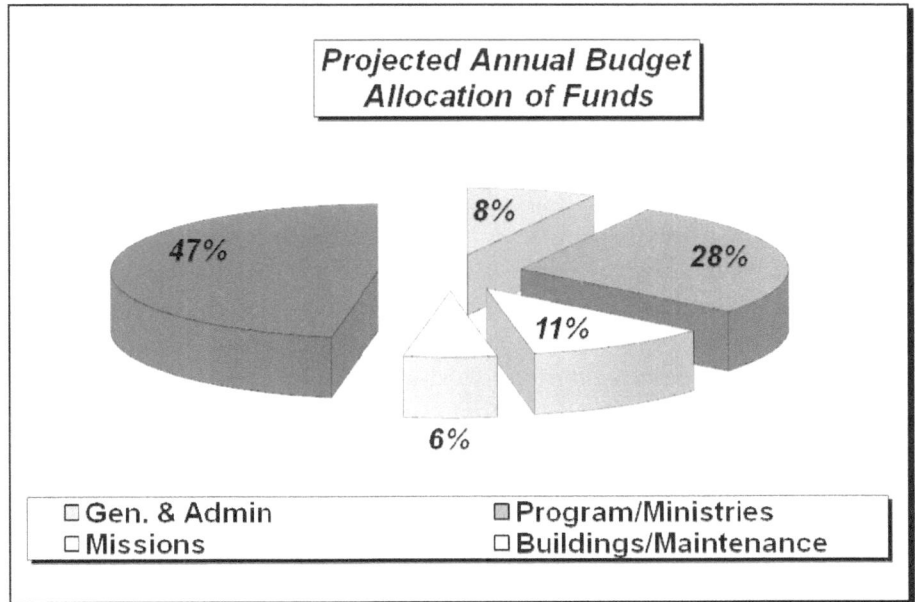

There are any numbers of ways the past and present budgets or financial reports can be presented. Again, the amount of information and the format will depend on the comfort level of the church leaders. Either the board "manages," or they "govern," and the level of information contained in the presentation will be determined by the governance philosophy.

We have at our disposal today all sorts of tools where we can make creative and interesting presentations. There is an old expression, "People give to what they can see." A building project with a model mock-up or an artist's rendering will get people's juices flowing faster than mere numbers on a page.

The same applies to the annual budget. Using images, videos, slides, and so forth, gets and holds people's attention more than printed handouts. Our culture is "visual," and ideas and concepts have more impact when more of our senses are incorporated.

Less is more! I personally believe that congregations should be moved toward accepting simplified summary budget presentations. Detailed financial statements are suitable for trustees or those charged with the oversight of the financial resources. In a larger setting, though, providing detailed budgets only invites public nit-picking. If the leadership of the church is selected based upon their *character* and *integrity*, then it usually follows that the supporters will trust their judgment and, more specifically, their budget projections. The goals should be to present ministry and not just money.

Assigned Line Items (Smaller Church)
Christian Education #200
Annual Budget

		2009 Actual	*2010 Projected Revenue*
Revenue			
3322	Camps	0000	0000
3352	Banquets	0000	0000
Total Revenue		00000	0000
Expenses			
4414	Salaries/Benefits	00000	00000
4420	Literature/Curriculum	000	000
4422	Camps	000	000
4572	Banquets	000	000
Total Expenses		$000,000	$000,000
Net Cost Operating Fund		$0,000	$0,000

Assigned Lined Items (Larger Church)
Youth Ministries #202s
Annual Budget

Revenue		2009 Actual	2010 Projected
3322	Camps/Retreats	00,000	00,000
3323	Short-Term Missions	0,000	0,000
Total Revenue		00,000	0,000
Expenses			
6202	Staff Compensation	$00,000	$00,000
6022	Camps/Retreats	00,000	00,000
6623	Short-Term Missions	0,000	0,000
6627	Supplies	0,000	0,000
6628	Curriculum	0,000	0,000
4429	Printing	000	000
4430	IT/Tech	000	000
4430	Staff Retreat (Full cost)	000	000
Total Expenses		$000,000	$00,000
	Net Cost Operating Fund	$00,000	$00,000

1. E. Peterson, *The Message* (Colorado Springs, CO: NavPress, 1995).

SHORTFALLS

When the Bottom Drops Out!

On December 30, 2009, members of Southern California's Saddleback Church, one of the largest in the country, received a shocking e-mail from Pastor Rick Warren.

With roughly 10 percent of the twenty-two-thousand-member congregation out of work, costs of caring for the church's Orange County community had risen dramatically. But income was stagnant.

Saddleback was able to stay on budget through prudent financial planning, Warren wrote, until "the bottom dropped out" at post-Christmas services.

"On the last weekend of 2009, our total offerings were less than half of what we normally receive," wrote Warren, "leaving us $900,000 in the red for the year, unless you help make up the difference today and tomorrow."

Members responded with $2.4 million in last-minute donations. But Saddleback's case, although certainly on an above-average-size scale, it nevertheless points to the precarious circumstances for many churches, which, like some in their congregations, live paycheck to paycheck.

A report released in early 2010 by the Barna Group, a research group focusing on faith and culture, found that budgets for Protestant churches were down about 7 percent on average from the year before. One in eleven churches lost 20 percent or more in annual income, with 2 percent reporting drops of 35 percent.

While you may be reading this years after the 2010 expected publishing date, the lessons learned from these reports remain constant. That is, declines in giving come as Americans pull back in large numbers from gifts to nonprofit groups in general and not just limited exclusively to churches.

Furthermore, this isn't a new problem, according to Scott Thumma of the Hartford Institute for Religion Research, who said donations to megachurches were basically flat between 2005 and 2008.

"So it wasn't a rosy picture even then," he said. "When we look at those same things in 2010, I think we'll see that it's been a decade of trouble for the church, a whole lot of trouble."

You may not personally be involved in a huge megachurch, but the pressure point of a shortfall in donations can cause some very challenging conditions and hard choices in churches of all sizes.

So what could church leaders do when deficits begin—when the outgo exceeds the inflow?

Communicating the Need

In an article in *Your Church*, a publication of Christianity Today, the issue of addressing a shortfall was discussed.

The letter from the board of an affluent midsized congregation in suburban Chicago contained an urgent message: increase giving or else.

While affirming the past faithful giving of members, the letter also emphasized the impact of the economic recession. Some members recently lost jobs and struggled to maintain their regular giving levels. And others who worried about their financial futures did not increase giving. The result: the church budget faced a serious and unexpected deficit, prompting the board to consider serious cuts in mission and ministry.

"We are striving to fulfill God's call, and also to be good stewards of your financial support to this church," the letter read. "Now, at this critical time in this ministry, we will have to make cuts in our staffing and programs. We know you do not want to see this happen. We know that you want us to meet our budget commitments. So we are asking you to give sacrificially and give more—as much as you can, right now—so that we can keep our ministry intact."

The church's pastor also preached a sermon on sacrificial giving. Lay leaders made their appeal at announcement times in the service. Some members gave testimonies of how the Lord gave them the resources to give more in tough times.

The appeal worked—to some extent. But cuts still occurred, and the board resolved to prepare a "bare bones budget" for the next fiscal year.[1]

The church leaders in this situation thought that highlighting the state of affairs as they saw it or "to tell it like it is" is the best approach. But many believe such an approach, often used by churches during periods of economic struggle, is fundamentally flawed, looking at stewardship as a budget-driven program based on human scarcity rather than a spiritual growth opportunity grounded in God's abundant provision for all needs.

Perhaps the best approach would be to address the shortfall in a two-pronged method.

What to Say

Leaders and stewardship consultants say the worst message that financially struggling churches can send is one of desperation, frustration, or shame. Instead, the message must emphasize opportunity. When communicating a significant shortfall, experts advise church leaders to emphasize what God can do through generous giving. The message should be crafted showing members how their giving produces tangible results. Most people today can't get too enthused about giving to a church's operational needs when they themselves are having difficulty meeting their own household needs. So the "outcomes" of their donations should be stressed instead of the fact that the church's budget isn't being met. People in general understand the fact that the church's budget isn't being met when it's obvious what's happening in their own lives and hear what is on the evening news.

There are those situations; of course, where local economic recessions aren't the reason giving is down. It isn't the intent of this book to examine issues of church splits, demographic changes, dissatisfaction with certain programs, and other negative impacts.

The important point at the heart of a financial need is the opportunity to promote spiritual growth in stewardship. This is not a comfortable topic for many pastors. In fact, according to one survey, 85 percent of pastors have little or no theological training in Christian stewardship and feel uncomfortable addressing the topic. This is too bad because cultivating and encouraging a generous spirit in the church makes a lot of sense if church leaders believe they serve a generous God, but they are reluctant in encouraging their people to give according to God's provision.

Jim Sheppard, principal partner and chief executive at Generis, a Christian stewardship and development firm, has said, "Now, we are in leaner times. Now we have to think and pray more deeply about the nature of the projects, and only the best will get funded because people will give the funding to those ministries with the best return on investment."

"In healthy churches, leaders never communicate that the economy is ransacking the church budget or causing massive cuts," Sheppard says. "Instead, they stress that God is opening many opportunities for ministry, and that God continues to bless people with resources to share."

Church leaders can take a twofold communications approach to prudent fiscal management and the promotion of generosity in giving. The fiscal budget acts as a solid financial planning tool, but church leaders also can develop a "dream budget" that spells out how the church's ministry can expand and grow with greater abundance—what it believes God has called it to do were additional resources to materialize.

What to Do

I realize that even in those situations where the best efforts at communicating financial needs aren't enough and the church consistently faces negative cash flow situations, the best action to take is to consider and reorganize their overall cash flow-management approach.

First—and this may sound like hindsight, but it really isn't—readjust your cash flow projections. Yes, that may mean cutting the budget or expenses—and we'll get to that in a moment—but I also suggest being proactive about contacting your creditors. I am always concerned about a church's reputation in a local community since creditors are people too and not just faceless names on bills and invoices. If you think you can't pay a bill on time, call and ask for an extension or explain that you're forced to make partial payment now with the balance coming in a few weeks. Your ability to do business depends upon your earning and sustaining other people's trust. If you can't have perfect credit, being honest and forthright is the next best thing to do. Yes, it's difficult and may feel embarrassing, but think of the alternative—not meeting your obligation to repay a business for what they provided to you in good faith.

When you must put off paying creditors, don't forget to include federal, state, and local tax agencies on the list of organizations to notify. Just because they are distant and bureaucratic doesn't mean that you shouldn't make personal contact. Fees and interest on unpaid taxes add up quickly. Setting up a payment plan, both over the phone and in writing, can prevent your assets from being frozen. Now how embarrassing is that? How you handle your creditors reflects on your church and, ultimately, the cause of Christ.

Small businesses, other nonprofit organizations, missionaries, and independent contractors are creditors who are the least likely to hassle you about late bill payments or to charge you interest. They are also in the weakest position to absorb late payments and bad debts. Don't overlook their needs and potential vulnerability.

Leaders who are in tune with the finances should know where reductions can be made to reduce expenses. Without me knowing the specifics of a church's line-by-line budget, there are nevertheless three general areas where cutbacks should be considered.

Staffing

Trim down staff by eliminating positions, not filling vacated positions, or modifying plans to hire new staff. As painful as this may be, it is the quickest way to reduce costs. Layoffs and salary reductions can be used to improve cash flow, which is an obvious solution. But again, take into consideration the effect this will have on not just the output of work on a daily basis, but also on the message it sends to the congregation. It should be viewed as necessary and being done reluctantly and not perceived as being impulsive or callous.

Programs

Postpone starting any new program especially if you've just made staff reductions. New activities or programs should be reconsidered in light of the economic conditions.

Services

Services that are provided by the church that have costs connected to them should be reevaluated. To repeat, this should be done carefully, considering the message it communicates, either positive or negative.

Always remember that this is a church environment where, for the most part, income is a result of people's faith conviction and generosity. Keep in mind that each of these strategies can result in the church compromising its mission if care is not taken and should be considered when there are no other alternatives. It's not always about dollars and cents; perception plays a very important role in how and what is done to reduce costs.

1. ChristianityToday.com, Your Church, 2009.

Special Events

Who Gets Credit?

One of the tremendous privileges granted to churches by federal and state governments is tax exemption for an individual's contributions. The right to receive a deduction from a person's taxes is a liberty not granted by other countries. A tax deduction is typically available to a donor to encourage them to make a gift for charitable purposes. However, like any privilege, there is a corresponding responsibility attached to it. One of those duties is to ensure certain donations are granted legally, and this is where pressure points can mount.

I speak from personal experience on this issue, for when it comes to what is and what is not permissible as a tax deduction, things can get very sticky! Fund-raising activities outside the offering collection plate can be a minefield of challenges. Auctions, fund-raising banquets, golf tournaments, Christian school tuition, camps, and retreats—all have the potential to spark tricky tax-deductibility issues.

Quid Pro Quo: What Is That?

January is the time when your churches need to begin the process of sending receipts to your donors for their contributions during the preceding tax year. There is one area in this regard that is often confusing. That has to do with what the Internal Revenue Service refers to as quid pro quo disclosure requirements. To help you understand this issue more clearly and to have an authoritative source for these comments and recommendations, I will be using as my source information gained from Daniel Busby, CPA, president of the Evangelical Council for Financial Accountability.

OK, so just what is quid pro quo, and what does it have to do with your church? It's a Latin phrase meaning "something for something." A quid pro quo contribution is a payment made partly as a contribution and partly for goods or services provided to the donor by the church (your church). A donor may deduct only the amount of the contribution above what the goods or services are worth.

Then what does this have to do with your church, and why is it important to know about it? Well, when a donor receives goods or services of value that is *equal* to or close to its value, there is *no gift*. This amount "given" isn't really a donation and tax deductible. This is because the person received a quid pro quo, again something for something, in exchange for the transfer; and thus, there is no gift at all. If the payment to your church *exceeds* the approximate amount of goods or services provided to the "payer," the difference qualifies as a charitable gift.

Your church is required to provide a receipt for all transactions where the donor makes a payment of more than $75 to the church and receives goods and services other than intangible or what's considered religious-in-nature benefits or items of token value. Since many, if not all, of the services you provide (e.g., marriage counseling) are free to your members, any donation they may offer in return is not subject to this rule.

Form of the Receipt

The receipt must inform your donor that the amount of the contribution that is deductible for federal income purposes is limited to the difference in the amount of money and the value of any property contributed by the donor over the value of goods and services provided by your church and provide the donor with a good faith estimate of the value of goods and services that the church is providing in exchange for the contribution.

There is at least some good news as it relates to this requirement. Only single payments of more than $75 are subject to the rules. Payments are not cumulative. It is not a difference of $75 between the amount given by the donor and the value of the object received by the donor that triggers the disclosure requirements, but the amount actually paid by the donor.

Calculating the Gift Portion

It is not a requirement for your church to actually complete the subtraction of the benefit from a cash payment, showing the net charitable deduction. However, providing the net amount available for a charitable deduction is a good approach for clear communication with your donors.

When to Make the Required Disclosures

The disclosure of the value of goods or services provided to a donor may be made up front when you solicit funds or payments, as well as in the subsequent receipt. However, you won't always know in advance when you're asking for funds what the value will be in order to make a proper disclosure. For example, the value of a fund-raising banquet dinner may not be known at the time of the solicitation. Making a good faith estimate is the best method in this case.

Goods Provided to Donors

To determine the net contribution, a gift must generally be reduced by the fair market value of the premium, incentive, or other benefit received by the donor in exchange for the gift. Common examples of premiums are books, CD/DVDs, or other items. For gifts of over $75, churches must advise the donor of the fair market value of the premium or incentive and explain that the value is not deductible for tax purposes.

Donors must reduce their charitable deduction by the fair market value of goods or services they receive even when the goods or services were donated to the church. Therefore, churches cannot pass along to donors the savings realized by receiving products at no cost or buying products at a discount.

If donors received benefits of less than $75, they are allowed a full tax deduction for the donation:

Low-cost items. **(Low-cost items must be free to the donor and "low-cost" to the distributing church or the church on whose behalf the item is distributed.)** If an item has a cost (not retail value) of less than $9.10 and such an item that bears the name or logo of your organization is given in return for a donation of more than $45.50 (2008 inflation—adjusted amount based on revenue procedure 2007-66), the donor may claim a charitable deduction for the full amount of the donation. Examples of items that often qualify as tokens are coffee mugs, key chains, bookmarks, and calendars. Complicated? Yes, I know, but I need to include this in case there is an IRS agent reading this section!

If a ministry sends unsolicited low-cost items at no charge to the donor as part of a fund-raising effort, donors are not required to make a deduction from the amount contributed (revenue procedure 92-49).

De minimis benefits. (Another one of those legalese words!) A donor can take a full deduction if the fair market value of the benefits received in connection with a gift does not exceed 2 percent of the donation or $91 (2008 inflation—adjusted amount), whichever is less.

Examples of the Quid Pro Quo Rules

Here are a few examples of how quid pro quo rules apply:

Admission to events. Many churches sponsor banquets, concerts, or other events to which donors and prospective donors are invited in exchange for a contribution or other payment. Often, the donor receives a benefit equivalent to the payment, and no charitable deduction is available.

Auctions. The IRS generally takes the position that the fair market value of an item purchased at a church auction is set by the bidders. The winning bidder, therefore, cannot pay more than the item is worth. That means that there is no charitable contribution in the IRS's eyes, no deduction, and no need for the church to provide any charitable gift substantiation documentation to the bidder.

However, many tax professionals take the position that when the payment (the purchase price) exceeds the fair market value of the items, the amount that exceeds the fair market value is deductible as a charitable contribution. This position also creates a reporting requirement under the quid pro quo rules. Most churches set the value of every object sold and provide receipts to buyers.

Example: Your church auctions items to raise funds for your short-term mission project. An individual bought a quilt for $200. The church takes the position that the quilt had a fair market value of $50 even though the bidder paid $200. Since the payment exceeded the $75 limit, the church is required to provide written statement indicating that only $150 of the $200 payment is eligible for a charitable contribution.

Bazaars. Payments for items sold at bazaars and bake sales are not tax deductible to donors since the purchase price generally equals the fair market value of the item.

Banquets. Whether your church incurs reporting requirements in connection with banquets where funds are raised depends on the specifics of each event.

Example 1: Your church sponsors a banquet charging $50 per person. The meal costs the church $15 per person. There is no disclosure requirement since the amount charged was less than $75. However, the amount deductible by each donor is only $35.

Example 2: Your church invites individuals to attend a fund-raising banquet without charge. Attendees are invited to make contributions or pledges at the end of the banquet. These payments probably do not require disclosure even if the amount given is $75 or more because there is only an indirect relationship between the meal and the gift.

One more comment: *Good faith estimates.* Your donor is not required to use the estimate you may have provided in calculating the deductible amount. When a donor knows or has reason to know that an estimate is inaccurate, the taxpayer may ignore the organization's estimate.

The following are sample receipts for use with church auctions.

CHURCH AUCTION
For Items *Purchased at the Auction*

Acknowledgment of Payment

Received from:_____ Date: _____

Address:_____

City:_____ State:_____ Zip: _____

Amount paid for auction item(s) $_____ (excludes sales tax)

Description and condition of items that were purchased at the auction:

Generally, the amount you paid for the auctioned items you received (described above) represents the fair market value of the item(s), resulting in no charitable deduction. In a few unusual situations, the amount that you paid for the auction item(s) may represent an excess of fair market value; and therefore, the excess amount may be deductible for federal and state income tax purposes (we will provide an estimated fair market value in these instances). Please consult with your own financial or tax advisor for more details.

Receipt issued by:

_____

Representative's Signature

Community Church, 111 Main Street, Any Town, CA 91235

COMMUNITY CHURCH AUCTION
For Items Donated *to the Auction*

Charitable Gift Receipt

Received from:_____ Date: _____

Address:_____

City:_____ State:_____ Zip: _____

Description and condition of items donated for the auction:

Please consult with your own financial or tax advisor to determine if you are eligible for a charitable donation deduction and, if so, the amount that may be claimed.

Our church did not provide any goods or services in exchange for this gift.

For gifts of $250 or more, this document is necessary to substantiate your gift. Please retain it for your records.

Receipt issued by:

_____

Representative's Signature

Community Church, 111 Main Street, Any Town, CA 91235

GUIDELINES OF COMPASSION

Assisting the Needy

Former president Reagan once proposed, "If every church and synagogue in the U.S. would adopt ten poor families beneath the poverty level, we could eliminate government welfare in this country." While this may no longer be true due to the higher numbers of those considered below the poverty level, he does make an interesting point.

Former New York City mayor Edward Koch once asked 350 churches and synagogues of his city to shelter ten homeless men and women each night. His proposal was criticized by priests, rabbis, and ministers. He received only seven positive replies.

Nearly two decades ago, a *Wall Street Journal* article spotlighted the situation. It stated that churches throughout the country faced increasing demands to help the impoverished. This dilemma is a growing concern among American congregation to this day.

The challenge to church leaders is clear: We need to respond biblically. We simply cannot sidestep the issue, leaving the care of the poor entirely up to the government and hoping it will go away. It hasn't and won't. It's here—at our doorstep.

Needy people will call the church, arrive in broken-down cars, or walk in the front door. They all have the same requests: food, a place to sleep, clothing, in some cases, or gasoline. Church members through their networks of friends become aware of a family whose father or mother has been unemployed for an extended period of time and for whatever reason doesn't have enough food for his family.

Historically, this was once the church's responsibility—providing aid to the poor, aged, and disabled. But the church, for whatever reasons, allowed government to take over this burden. Now because of cuts in various federal—and state-funded assistance programs, people are again turning to the church for help.

Although there is an expectation that churches should care for the needy, most congregations are not prepared to cope. They either have limited resources or simply do not feel obligated to help the poor.

The church has three options:

1. *Help everyone.* Provide food, shelter, and clothing to anyone who can demonstrate an apparent need and then allow God to deal with the question of their "honesty."
2. *Help no one.* The philosophy of "we four—no more—shut the door" is unfortunately typical in many of today's church. Parishioners believe that the problem is beyond the ministry's "mission statement" and scope of the local church. After all, "don't we pay taxes to support the government programs for the needy?"
3. *Help the truly needy.* The ideal is to help these people become self-sufficient without creating a dependency on the church to become just another welfare system.

In aiding the poor, we need to answer three questions to develop unambiguous policy.

Who Qualifies for Aid?

The Bible classifies two types of individuals. Hebrew 13:2 tells us, "Do not neglect to show hospitality to strangers, for by this some have entertained angels without knowing it." Also, in 1 John 3:17, we read, "Whosoever has the world's goods, and sees his brother in need and closes his heart against him, how does the love of God abide in him?"

Therefore, we are responsible to help strangers and those in Christ's body. In setting priorities, the scripture tells us to "do good to all men, and especially to those who are of the household of the faith" (Galatians 6:10). Our first obligation, therefore, is to God's redeemed family.

Whom Do We Consider Needy?

Generally speaking, we need to respond to those without resources or an immediate ability to help themselves. In 1 Timothy 5:5, it describes needy widows as destitute, lacking a means for support. They're the ones devoid of basic necessities, "without clothing and in need of daily food" (James 2:15).

Resources include assistance from family, relatives, and friends (1 Timothy 5:4). This would be the first "ring" in the circle of responsibility—immediate family and then friends, if possible. A case can be made that basic resources would not include holding on to property, savings accounts, cars, televisions, or any other surplus items that can be exchanged for basic services. The bar is set pretty low when considering a person's genuine need. But it has to be if you are going to assist everyone who comes forth with a "need." Where do you draw the line? That would be up to the leadership of the church, but I have suggested a starting point as a basis for the definition of neediness.

People worthy of aid, therefore, are those lacking necessities or the immediate ability to remedy their situation.

To What Extent Should We Meet Needs?

The answer, although simple to say, is difficult to implement. We have to meet immediate needs while helping individuals become self-supporting. Giving food without guidance encourages people to return whenever they get hungry. But there are many practical solutions.

Church members can donate nonperishable food items, clothing, and blankets for the needy. Gift certificates purchased from local supermarkets or fast-food restaurants also help.

One way to handle a difficult situation, especially if it's a man, is to allow him to work for his money. The Bible says if a man won't work, he should not eat (2 Thessalonians 3:10). Exercise caution when dealing with strangers, but in principle, handing a man a paintbrush or shovel is a sure way to check out his motivation!

The local church can use public agencies, usually funded by private donors, to help those outside the congregation. The Salvation Army, rescue missions, halfway houses, and other organizations are equipped to aid the distressed. In many areas, churches help regional food banks through direct donations or volunteering their services on a regular basis.

When money is given, it must be handled carefully. Cash might not be used for its intended purpose. Examine the validity of each person's request. Therefore, it is wise to have an established policy and procedure for providing assistance. It is best to have a list of questions in the form of a questionnaire to be filled out by the person requesting aid.

It's obvious due to the overwhelming amount of need that American churches cannot completely replace the nation's welfare system. The government also should not throw its poor on to the local church, saying, "Here, we can't afford these people anymore. You take them." That's simply not realistic. However, we are committed to helping the truly needy when we can and to help them where possible to be self-sufficient. That includes spiritual food as well as physical sustenance. Let's not neglect this aspect of our "aid program" by pouring all our time and resources into only meeting physical needs. In quoting the Old Testament, Jesus said, "Man shall live by bread alone, but every word that proceeds out of the mouth of God" (Matthew 4:4).

The following sample questionnaire and benevolence policy are provided merely as a guideline or starting point. Clearly, you would want to design your own policies and procedures to fit your specific circumstance and capabilities.

Sample
Request for Assistance Questionnaire
Mountain Community Church

1. Are you are a church member? If not, how were you referred to us?

2. What is your need? (Please be specific.)

3. Where do your closest relatives live?

4. Do they know about your need?

5. Are you receiving aid (financial or otherwise) from a government agency like Aid to Families with Dependent Children (AFDC) and Women, Infants and Children (WIC) aid, food stamps, unemployment insurance, social security, or worker's compensation benefits?

6. Have you been employed locally? Where?

7. When and where was the last time you sought employment?

8. Are you willing to work today if we know of an available job?

9. Do you attend church? If so, where?

10. What is your minister's name? Does he know of your need?

11. Have you sought assistance at any other churches in this area? If so, where?

12. If we are unable to help you, what other options do you have?

13. If we are able to help you, how many people are involved? (Please list family members or dependents.)

14. Do you have some form of identification?

15. May I have permission to take your photograph for identification purposes?

(Please remember, our church is not a government-assisted agency. All available resources are a result of direct donations from our congregation and may be limited in their amount.)

Sample
Benevolence Policy
Mountain Community Church

Church members can receive assistance as often as the deacons handling these needs feel is necessary.

Nonmembers can be assisted no more that quarterly.

The Request for Assistance Questionnaire checklist must be followed.

The dollar level of the assistance should follow the guidelines outlined in the policy.

Cash

No cash is to be given to anyone. Checks will be written to respective utilities, landlords, etc.

The person being helped will be responsible for providing all telephone and account numbers necessary to receive the credit on their account and not rely on church staff to do this.

Automobile Fuel

Cash is to be taken by the staff member or deacon to the nearest gas station of his choice, and he/she pays for the fuel.

A maximum of $10 is allowed for fuel purchases.

Prescriptions

If prescription assistance is given, generic drugs are to be first choice.

Assistance will not be provided for potentially habit-forming drugs such as Tylenol no. 3, Hydrocodone, Xanax, Soma, etc. If exceptions are to be made, an attempt to contact a physician in the church should be made first to verify the need.

Emergency Shelter

Nonmembers
Staff members are to refer to the listing of housing shelters as a first priority. (A listing of shelters should be prepared and printed for each staff member and available in the church office.)

If no shelter can be secured—and as a last resort—housing at a local motel may be provided under the following guidelines:

- a maximum of two nights Sunday through Thursday
- a maximum of three nights Friday through Sunday

Members
Housing should be sought with another family in the church.

Utilities, Telephone, and Rent

Members
The allowed amount is to be determined by the deacons on an individual situation-by-situation basis.

Nonmembers
The maximum allowable amount is $50.

No funds are to be provided for deposit money.

Checks are to be written directly to the utility company or the landlord. Checks are mailed from the church office to the utility or landlord or hand carried by a staff member.

No rent is given when the landlord is a family member or a relative of the person requesting assistance.

All rent requests are to be investigated by contacting the landlord before assistance is granted.

Telephone assistance is for the amount of the monthly charge. No long-distance charges are to be paid.

Food

Members
The allowed amount is $50 unless authorized for more by the deacon in charge.

The church pantry should be utilized before funds are provided.

Food gift certificates for local grocery stores may be used in $50 increments or less. These are to be imprinted with wording that they are not to be used for alcohol or tobacco products.

Nonmembers
The maximum limit is $25.

Food gift certificates for a fast-food restaurant may be issued in emergency situations. (A small supply should be kept on hand at all times and to be used *only* for the purpose of assistance to the *needy*.)

Identification Required

For nonmembers receiving assistance, a photo ID is required before assistance involving money or gift certificates are given.

CONCLUSION

A final thought.

In confronting and dealing with the pressure points of church finances, there is a single overarching principle we must keep in mind. It's best embodied in the phrase "We just work here!" We're called God's servants, and we're told it's required of us that we "prove faithful" (1 Corinthians 4:2). We should keep that in mind when we set our budgets and manage the money. Let's not have an inflated view of our own value. We don't own the store, we just work here!

Randy Alcorn in his book *The Treasure Principle* describes this responsibility in a clever illustration. Suppose you have something important you want to get to someone who needs it. You wrap it up and hand it over to the FedEx guy. What would you think if instead of delivering the package, he took it home, opened it, and kept it for himself? You'd say, "This guy doesn't get it. The package doesn't belong to him. He's just the middleman. His job is to get it from me to the person I want him to hand it off to." Likewise, we are like the delivery guy. What we have, the God-given financial resources don't belong to us. We are to "deliver" the resources to further His kingdom. We are managers of His money, not owners—delivery people not recipients. We are to manage His treasure for His purposes until the day when He returns.

> *Moreover, it is required of stewards that they be found faithful* (1 Corinthians 4:2).

INDEX